# LATIN AMERICA
## *today* and *tomorrow*

# LATIN

## *today*

# AMERICA

## and
## *tomorrow*

### by GALO PLAZA Lasso

*Secretary General, Organization of American States*

*published by*
## acropolis books ltd.

WASHINGTON, D.C. / 20009

**ACROPOLIS BOOKS LTD.**
Colortone Building, 2400 17th St., N.W.
Washington, D.C. 20009

Printed in the United States of America by
Colortone Creative Graphics Inc., Washington, D.C. 20009

Type set in Ultima and Sans
by Colortone Typographic Division, Inc.

Design by Design and Art Studio 2400, Inc.

**Library of Congress Catalog Number 73-148677**

Standard Book No. 8749-135-4

# CONTENTS

# INTRODUCTION

For years I have felt that too many Americans take Latin America for granted.

They have little conception of the magnitude of the self-help effort of the Latin American countries to improve the quality of life of their people, or of the internal and external obstacles to the achievement of that objective.

They do not understand why it is in the best interest of the United States and the rest of the developed world to co-operate in that effort, or what types of cooperation are most needed.

Finally, they do not understand the many-faceted role of the Organization of American States, in which the United States and Latin America have pledged themselves to a united effort to ensure social justice and economic development throughout the Americas, as conditions essential to peace and security.

To these Americans—to students, government officials, factory workers, housewives, and businessmen who are willing to invest a couple of hours of their time to become better informed about Latin America—this little book is directed.

I have endeavored to present, as clearly as possible, the facts about what is really going on in Latin America, and why this is of importance to the United States. I am convinced that the more widely these facts become known, the firmer will be this country's commitment to its partnership with Latin America.

My observations are those of a Latin American who has spent several years in the United States—first as a student, then as a diplomat, and most recently as Secretary General of the Organization of American States. I know the American people. Given the facts, I believe they will no longer take Latin America for granted.

—Galo Plaza

*Latin America is known for rapid population growth and the youthful profile of its people. Ecuadorian school children.*

*Self-help housing projects
offer new hope
to millions of
Latin Americans. Project in Chile.*

# CHAPTER I

# CONTINENT OF CHANGE

Every country of Latin America has its distinctive profile. But all have one thing in common: they are in the throes of transformation, more pervasive, dramatic, and fundamental than at any other time in history. Change in Latin America is of course only part of the worldwide pattern, but it is quicker, more radical, more explosive, and more permeated with ideology. This dynamism may be discomforting to those who do not really understand it, but it is by and large constructive and creative.

Contrary to stereotype, there has always been change in Latin America, as indeed everywhere else in the Western World. What is different now is the pace of change, and the prospect that it will come faster and faster, affecting every part of the social fabric: personal values, morality, religion, and, especially, politics and economics.

After more than a century and a half of national independence, the Latin American countries are still in the process of developing their political institutions to serve this integral development. Let us not forget that the Latin American countries of the nineteenth century were little more than outposts of European and American culture. But imported political patterns were often inconsistent with the Latin American reality. This factor may have contributed to delay the present vigorous spurt of development, conceived in terms of economic growth plus social justice.

At the risk of over-simplifying, one could say that the prime engine of change in contemporary Latin America is one of the region's greatest assets: the people.

Latin America is young. Fifty-three percent of the region's people are less than 20 years old. Each year some 2.5 million young people join the labor force and become eligible to vote. Each year some 2 million young people flock to the cities to seek their fortunes, crowding together in the sprawling slums of our great cities, where they become increasingly aware of social injustice, cultural backwardness, a lack of economic advance and opportunity. The demonstration effect is devastating. They learn to aspire to a new life, becoming aware of the fact that it is within their power to advance toward their goals, and that only tradition—or inertia—stands between them and fulfillment.

The Church in Latin America has been a force for social change and structural reform for some time, especially under the inspiration of Pope John. Today, it is an integral part of the Latin American transformation; and there is reason to believe that it will provide in the near future a more powerful ideological force toward reform than many of the imported ''isms.''

The forces of change generated by the people of Latin America are no mere imitation of a foreign original. There is a growing awareness in our region that political and economic development depend essentially on internal effort, national ideals and traditions, and local customs and institutions.

From the vantage point of the United States or European public it may often appear as if Latin America were now engaged in a simple process of taking sides between East and West, that is to say between oversimplified, overpolarized positions in the cold war, or between the dogmas of either free enterprise or statism. Latin America balks at this false dilemma and shies away from any all-out traditional ideological identification.

Latin America is experiencing a kind of Hegelian synthesis between various doctrines and ideologies, which are being selectively adapted to national requirements. As the measure of popular participation in the shaping of society increases, through education and mass media of communication, the countries of Latin America are emerging into integrated nationhood.

Latin America more and more looks toward Europe and other continents for mutually beneficial relations to parallel those our countries have had with one another and with the United States. In this sense, Latin America is not, nor will it ever be, the private domain or the backyard of any power.

There is a widespread tendency in some quarters to lump Latin America together with the so-called "Third World," assumed to extend to all developing, non-industrialized countries, most of which happen to be south of the Equator. Latin America, however, is not truly a part of the Third World; it is the bridge to it. It is the only viable intermediary, not tainted with the rancid taste of colonialism, between the United States and Western Europe on the one hand, and the Afro-Asian bloc on the other. The average per capita income of Latin America is over three times that of Africa and Asia. The per capita GNP of the larger countries in our region comes close to that of many highly industrialized nations. The future course of Latin American development may provide the pattern for that of other regions of the developing world.

Latin America—a developing region on its way to industrialization—is as much a part of the Western community, whose cultural background it shares and in whose heritage it is steeped, as any less industrialized part of Western Europe, such as Portugal, Spain, Greece, Finland, or the Italian *Mezzoggiorno*. In only two decades the Latin American market will have roughly the same income and market possibilities as the European Economic Community today, even at the still rather modest growth rate of the past ten years.

Over the past five years or so the countries of Latin America, regardless of their individual forms of government, have gradually developed a new unity of purpose and posture vis-a-vis the outside world. Latin America has stopped being a sphere of influence; it is now an influence in its own right, because it is united and certain of its own strength and potential.

Latin America can assume a much more influential stance internationally than heretofore because it has indeed undergone profound change in its economic development. As a region, it is on the threshold of take-off. At the national level, it has in some cases reached it and in others it is well on its way.

In 1969 Latin America had a real growth rate of its gross product of 5.7 percent, one of the highest during the past decade. While the average annual increase in per capita GDP for 1961-68 was 1.7 percent, the 1969 figure was 2.8 percent. For the second consecutive year since the beginning of the decade, the region reached the minimum per capita GDP growth rate of 2.5 percent that was established as a goal in the Charter of Punta del Este in 1961. This level was attained in more than half of the Latin American countries, including those with the largest population. More than 85 percent of Latin America's population in 1969 lived in countries where the GDP increased by over 5 percent. All indications are that these levels will be surpassed in 1970.

This encouraging performance was in large part due to the favorable markets for Latin America's traditional exports, underlining the importance of trade to the region's growth. The rise in exports is no longer used largely for sumptuary expenditures abroad as in the past. New progressive tax systems, better administered and enforced, improved economic management, and an increasingly dynamic private sector, all have combined to ensure that export earnings are channelled into productive economic uses and to improve social well-being. Rationalization of the fiscal apparatus and curbing of inflation in the major countries have been chiefly the result of their own efforts.

Even the most coldly pragmatic observer of Latin America today is struck by the stupendous vitality of the peoples of our region, by their great achievements in domesticating nature, their feats of engineering, and their massive efforts to build an infrastructure for the world of tomorrow.

Self-help has been the keynote to our development, and it has generated an introspective attitude, an alienation, a disaffection of youth, that can and should be remedied in favor of a broader perspective of interdependence.

The northern industrialized world can ill afford to be a passive bystander to the dynamic process of development taking place in Latin America today. Latin America wants and needs the developed world's cooperation, on terms that respect the region's freedom of action and enable it to improve the quality of life of its people.

*Plaza of
Three Cultures
in Mexico City surrounds
pre-Columbian and
colonial period
structures with
twentieth-century skyscrapers.*

Sculptures at entrance of headquarters
of Organization of American States
in Washington exemplify the contrast
between the Latin American spirit of
contemplation (left) and the North
American spirit of action (right).
These stereotypes no longer hold true.

# CHAPTER 2

# CULTURAL VALUES

Is there a Latin American way of feeling, thinking, and acting, coextensive with the region? No other region of the world has so many countries linked by language, religion, and cultural tradition, yet Latin America is a continent of contrasts. The Andean region, where the Indian's presence is so pervasive, is quite unlike the Atlantic coastal belt, with its big cities such as Buenos Aires and São Paulo, where immigrants from several nations have left their mark. The Caribbean region and northern South America receive a distinctive flavor from the African influence. Differences in physical geography and the historical development of separate and independent republics, some of which have at times been at odds with one another, have also served to foster diversity. However, the fact remains that much of what we today call Latin America shares the same general background. The spirit of unity is particularly strong in the five Central American countries, where a dynamic Common Market is in operation.

To understand Latin America's background we must look back almost five centuries, to the time of the Conquest. We must consider the values of the Indians, the values of the conquistadors, the effect of their clash, and their gradual fusion.

Unlike the primitive and generally nomadic Indians of the United States and Canada, the Indians to the south had developed advanced civilizations. The Aztecs' capital, Tenochtitlán, had a population greater than that of Madrid or even London at the time. The beauty of Tenochtitlán's architecture, as revealed today by a faithfully reconstructed model in the Museum of Anthropology in Mexico City, rivals anything that Europe could offer, then or now. Only in some of the Egyptian palaces do we find a comparable purity of line and simplicity of form—qualities for which contemporary architecture strives so greatly.

In South America, the Incas had developed social and political values as impressive as the remarkable physical constructions at Cuzco, Peru, which are the envy of engineers to this day.

The Incas set much store by matters of social conscience, and had a generous welfare system. Chieftains were required to put aside part of each community's crop for state purposes, including pensions for widows and orphans. When Inca legions once captured a maker of poisoned arrows that inflicted an agonizing death, the ruler had the opportunity to start producing the arrows for Inca use. He not only refused to adopt the weapon, but he prohibited anyone from using it, under penalty of death. The Inca believed that warfare should be as humane as possible, which is an indication of his high moral values.

The conquistadors from Spain and Portugal who changed the course of history in Latin America were not at all like the Pilgrims who were to settle in New England in the following century. The Pilgrims were *bona fide* colonists, looking for a new life of freedom, while the conquistadors were adventurers who planned to return to the mother country as soon as they had found their share of the New World's gold.

Another difference is the fact that the conquistadors did not bring their wives with them as the Pilgrims did, which explains the rapid miscegenation.

The conquistador had a firm concept of personal dignity and an equally firm dislike of manual labor. Unlike the Pilgrim fathers, who had a religious obsession with earning their bread by the sweat of their brows, and few qualms about driving the Indians off the land, the conquistadors preferred to force Indians to do the work. This marked the beginning of the rigid class lines and attitudes toward physical labor that are still somewhat of a problem today.

Side by side with the conquistadors came the priests and missionaries, whose zealous efforts to convert, educate, and protect the Indians had positive and far-reaching influence in the colonial period.

The effect of the Conquest is symbolized in the Square of Three Cultures in Mexico City. It is recorded there that the encounter between Cortez and the Aztec prince Cuauhtémoc ended in neither victory nor defeat but in the emergence of a new entity: the Mexican people.

In some instances the clash between two cultures before giving birth to a third was tragic. When a priest accompanying Pizarro told the Inca Atahualpa that he must swear by the Holy Bible, which was the word of God, the Inca put the book to his ear. "I can hear nothing," he replied. At that instant Pizarro ordered his troops to slaughter the Indians.

It is true that the Iberians imposed their cultural values during the Conquest, and that the Indians had to adapt themselves as best they could, but the adaptation was far from total. The Indian accepted European values with reservations. His attitude is exemplified in a charming anecdote in Garcilaso de la Vega's classic *Royal Commentaries*. Garcilaso tells of a marriage ceremony between a Spanish captain and an Inca princess. The princess and her royal family, with their hierarchical prejudices, were concerned about the fact that the Spanish captain had been a tailor before joining the army. When the priest asked "Do you take this man to be your lawful wedded husband?" the princess replied, in Quechua, *"Ichach munani, ichach mana munani,"* which means "Maybe I do, maybe I don't." This is the way many European customs and laws were received.

Over the centuries in Latin America there has been a great deal of blending and fusion of European, Indian, and in some areas African values. Nevertheless, there continue to be clearly discernible elements of diversity. Latin America has produced some of the most refined and brilliant writers in the Spanish and Portuguese languages, but at the same time there are still many communities where only Indian languages are heard. In the Andean regions we find consecrated crosses that bear on either side the symbols of the sun and moon—a holdover from pre-Columbian pagan cults. In Brazil we find the strange admixture of voodoo and Christian elements in the rites of the *macumba*.

One cultural characteristic in Latin America, inherited from both the Indians and the Mediterranean races, is a sense of beauty and respect for form. If we admire the stark lines of pre-Columbian work in gold and stone, we also appreciate the transformation which the European baroque underwent in the hands of the Indian craftsmen who built the Jesuit mission churches of Paraguay and fashioned the alterpieces of the great colonial churches in Mexico, Quito, and Cuzco, and in the hands of the Brazilian mulattoes who raised and carved the graceful shrines of Minas Gerais. The Latin American gift of aesthetic beauty extends to music as well, for Latin rhythms are played, sung, and danced all over the world.

Another basic Latin American characteristic derived from both the Indians and the Iberians is the emphasis on contemplation rather than action. The cultural anthropologist Kusch has pointed out that in Quechua the verb "to be" does not cover the concept of "becoming." In Quechua, "to be" means "to stay put." The Latin American has traditionally tended to have a static outlook, because for him time is an ever-recurring phenomenon, with no connotation of urgency. This is directly contrary to the dynamic concept expressed by the Anglo-Saxon saying "Time waits for no man."

For the contemplater *mañana* will recur. It will not disappear as it will for one who has a linear concept of time, in which the past is gone forever and the present is a fleeting moment between the past and the future. Therefore, when an American speaks derisively of a *mañana* attitude in Latin American culture, implying that things will inevitably be postponed, he is being unfair, although perhaps accurate from his own point of view.

Furthermore, the Latin American emphasis on diplomacy and courtesy tends to make us value the word more than the deed, and to think that resolutions constitute action. In contrast, there is the U.S. attitude that no problem is insoluble if appropriate resources are brought to bear. These traits naturally influence the formulation of inter-American policies and programs.

The contrast between the spirit of contemplation and the spirit of action is clearly illustrated in the large sculpture groupings at either side of the entrance to the OAS headquarters in Washington. One grouping, by Isidore Konti, represents South America; the other, by Gutzon Borglum, represents North America. Each grouping contains a mother and her adolescent son, symbolizing the youthful character of the New World. The mothers look into the distance. The sons look curiously at each other. The facial expressions on the South American figures are soft, pensive, dreamy, and sensuous. The North American figures, in sharp contrast, appear determined, alert, powerful, and restive.

These sculptures were done fifty years ago. Today values are undergoing a marked change. Urgent demands for economic and social development are forcing Latin America to move away from the contemplative attitude toward time. Today we feel compelled to act, to obtain the benefits of technology and to put our institutions in tune with the times. This is a key turning point in the evolution of Latin American cultural values.

But let us make no mistake. Our culture will demand a balance between this new sense of urgency and our traditional attitude of contemplation. We do not want to move ahead so fast and so far that we lose our capacity to enjoy the fruits of our labors. There must be a compromise between the dynamic drive toward technological improvement and the static resistance to alteration of those human values that make life worthwhile.

In this respect perhaps we Latin Americans can make a contribution to our neighbors, who are often too pressed by the urgency of linear time to be able to sit back and enjoy what life has to offer in terms of its graces, its beauty, and even its sensuality.

Perhaps North Americans would develop fewer ulcers if they spent more time in coffee bars, leisurely solving the world's problems and watching the girls go by. They also might enjoy life more—and protect their environment in the process— if they were more obsessed with beauty and less obsessed with consumption.

This is not to imply that most Latin Americans are erudite lovers of the arts and most North Americans are not. Stereotypes of this sort have been perpetuated for too long and should be rejected once and for all.

In the United States, despite the inroads of television on leisure time, people are buying more paper-back books in the drugstores and supermarkets than ever before, and are participating more actively than ever in amateur theatricals, music groups, and art and hobby activities.

On the other hand, in Latin America there is no hiding the fact that roughly half the adult population does not have the equivalent of a first-grade education. Schools are being built and teachers trained at record rates, but progress has largely been offset by the rapid growth of the population. It may be that a Latin American doctor is more widely read than his U.S. counterpart, as a result of the type of education he has had. But the sad truth is that the vast majority of Latin Americans do not read at all. Estimates made by the General Secretariat of the OAS and corroborated by other agencies on the basis of newspaper readership have come up with the shocking conclusion that only 6 percent of the adult literates of Latin America read books. There is a critical need for a vast quantity of easy-to-read materials for children and barely literate adults. Lack of these materials will result in the perpetuation of a large group of nominal literates who have actually lapsed back into illiteracy.

Statistics are scarce on library holdings and book circulation in Latin America, but isolated data reveal the general level of this cultural activity. Official Brazilian statistics indicate that in 1965, when Latin America's largest country had a population of 81,000,000, its public libraries contained about 15,000,000 volumes and their annual circulation was about 4,000,000. In other words, library loans averaged out to one for every twenty citizens. In that same year, in the United States, public libraries serving areas of 50,000 or more lent a total of 535 million books, or almost two and one-half books per capita. These figures are not as an indictment of Brazilian libraries, but proof of the fact that Brazilian readers, like those of the other Latin American countries, are few and far between.

In many Latin American countries the middle class is growing at a remarkable rate and is filling in the traditional gulf between the elite and the poverty-stricken. This is perhaps the most significant and most promising change that is taking place in the region. The middle class families have new interests, new responsibilities, and new opportunities.

Hundreds of thousands of new domestically produced cars

and motor scooters are having their inevitable effect on traditional patterns in work, leisure, and courting. An even more ubiquitous sign of the times in Latin America is the transistor radio. On the streets of nearly every village and town people walk by with their ears glued to radios, engrossed in a soccer game or the latest hit tune. Radio is being employed successfully as a weapon in the war on ignorance, but it is a double-edged sword that is encouraging wants and demands that cannot yet be fully satisfied.

Even the time-honored tradition of the siesta is fading. In Chile a few years ago the Government abolished the two-hour lunch period for public and private employees. Initial resistance to this drastic change is waning, especially among workers who enjoy spending less time commuting and more time with their families.

In Latin America today there is a new awareness of the interplay between the material and spiritual worlds. We realize that a culture that remains alien to the basic needs of its people is sterile and meaningless, and will wither away. But at the same time we know that man hungers for something more than food, clothing, medicine, and basic education. That is why both material and spiritual well-being are essential to our philosophy of development.

People in the United States are becoming more world-minded and more humanistic at the same time that we Latin Americans are becoming more pragmatic and given to specialization. Without abandoning any of the basic elements of our respective cultures, we are drawing closer together in outlook and attitudes. In spite of cultural and economic differences between the United States and Latin America there is a common dedication to freedom and peaceful development that draws us together.

What does it all mean? Where will the changing cultural values in Latin America lead? These new attitudes, new outlooks, and new approaches are elements in a long, invigorating process of evolution. The changes are welcome, and the people of Latin America are making the best of them as they push onward toward fulfillment of their historic mission, which, as stated in the preamble of the OAS Charter, is "to offer to man a land of liberty, and a favorable environment for the development of his personality and the realization of his just aspirations." In other words, the relevance of cultural change lies in its ability to help man improve his well-being and enjoy a fuller, more satisfying life. This is the challenge—and the opportunity—of cultural change.

*Majestic*
*Machu Picchu*
*is one of*
*Peru's principal*
*tourist attractions.*

*Presidents of
the Americas confer
at 1967 summit meeting
in Punta del Este, Uruguay.*

# CHAPTER 3

# INTER-AMERICAN RELATIONS

## OLD POLICIES WITH NEW TRIMMINGS?

Some may ask whether there are any new directions in inter-American relations. This is a legitimate question, not only from cynics but from thoughtful observers who feel that over the years inter-American relations have remained basically unchanged, and that the so-called new policies are actually old policies with new trimmings.

Some of the policies actually are quite old. The first President in the United States to instruct his diplomatic representatives in Latin America to respect the countries of that region as equals and to offer sincere cooperation and improved trade relationships was Abraham Lincoln. Even before Lincoln reached the Presidency, his voice in Congress sounded loud and clear in defense of Mexico, demanding respect for principles of international justice at a time when expansionist fever under the banner of "manifest destiny" was sweeping the United States.

Years later, in 1881, Secretary of State James G. Blaine's first invitation to the Latin American countries to attend the inter-American congress that eventually was held in 1889 said that the United States had no intention to appear as "the protector of its neighbors or the predestined arbitrator of their disputes." Blaine added that "the United States will enter into the deliberations of the Congress on the same footing as the other powers represented, and with the loyal determination to approach any proposed solution, not merely in its own interest, or with a view to asserting its own power, but as a single member among many coordinate and coequal states."

In the early decades of this century, of course, that coequal spirit was overshadowed by "dollar diplomacy" and the "big stick."

Then in the 1930's, when the cauldron of Europe began bubbling again, the United States adopted the Good Neighbor Policy to strengthen its ties to the south, and accepted the principle of nonintervention. But the Good Neighbor was in no position to extend large-scale financial cooperation in those post-depression years.

After the honeymoon relationship during the Second World War, U.S. interest in the economic development of Latin America was soft-pedaled as the United States assumed new responsibilities in other parts of the globe, and as the unquestioned assumption of the "safe neighborhood" in an otherwise threatening world became the basis of American policy for Latin America. At Bogotá in 1948 the experience of 58 years of collective inter-American relations was consolidated in the Charter of the OAS. While less newsworthy than the "Bogotazo," the disconcerting note struck by the United States delegation on economic policy reverberated in the conference deliberations almost as much. The spotlight was not focused on Latin American development until the start of the Alliance for Progress in 1961, which by some strange coincidence followed the establishment of the first communist government in the Americas.

But the Alliance for Progress, as we shall see, promised to accomplish too much too soon; sweeping institutional change anywhere is a slow and difficult process.

Progress was made, however, and Latin America's domestic investment in development far exceeded expectations. But in the United States presidential requests for appropriations to meet the U.S. commitment under the Alliance have been slashed with increasing severity by Congress as part of the general trend to cut back on foreign aid. The loans granted to Latin America were encumbered with restrictions. At the same time, Congress continued to favor protectionist trade policies that did not encourage expansion and diversification of Latin American exports.

In the light of these developments, it is not surprising that many have questioned the sincerity of the U.S. commitment to Latin America.

The revolution in communications and transportation has brought the United States and Latin America into closer proximity than ever before, to the point where it is impossible to ignore the need to strengthen cooperation. The problems are no longer remote; they are ringing in our ears. And with the general propensity to magnify bad news and minimize solid progress, the positive accomplishments must be strong indeed to make an impact. Every American knows what happens on the Sea of Tranquility, but how many know what is happening on the mighty Amazon, the River Plate, the Orinoco, or in the Caribbean?

We Latin Americans are chronically concerned about the fact that most citizens of the United States have a very fuzzy idea of what is going on in our part of the world. Our attitude is only human; it does not stem from any deep-seated feelings of inferiority or superiority. We realize that the United States' responsibilities are worldwide and we do not expect every American to be an expert on Latin America. All the same, we feel that too many Americans still think of Latin America only in terms of sombreros, siestas, and Chiquita Banana.

Even among those who are more familiar with Latin America by study, travel, or professional contact there is a great deal of misunderstanding. One of the most common tendencies is underestimation of the magnitude of the Latin American self-help effort. It is not generally known that of the estimated $130 billion invested in Latin American development in the sixties, a little over $120 billion is reckoned to have come from Latin America itself. Although the proportion of external aid was less than the 20 percent envisaged under the Alliance for Progress, it did play an important role in human and material betterment in Latin America.

Some Latin Americans—the ultra-nationalists—believe that every step the United States takes, or fails to take, is part of a sinister campaign of domination and exploitation. Suspicion of U.S. motives in belatedly supporting Latin American integration movements is an example. Most Latin Americans recognize that the age of "the big stick" is past, and view U.S. cooperation more objectively, but they feel that the United States is still not acting in Latin America's best interests, when it does such things as prohibit the spending of U.S. assistance for

The dedication
of the
Pan American
Union building
on April 26, 1910.

purchases outside the Hemisphere, and discourage Latin American exports. Few indeed are the Latin Americans who do not have some reservations with respect to the U.S. commitment to aid economic and social development in the region.

In the United States large sectors of public opinion have no opinion whatever on inter-American relations, because they receive little or no information on Latin America. In view of the difficulty in covering day-to-day progress in a score of countries, the press for the most part limits its coverage to natural disasters and changes of government. This highly literate nation is singularly uninformed about Latin America. For example, many Americans are ignorant of the fact that Brazil accounts for one-third of Latin America's population and that its people speak Portuguese rather than Spanish. Of course, Brazilians and their neighbors can usually understand one another, because so many of the words in their languages are similar or identical, but sometimes the similarity is deceptive. For example, *exquisito* in Spanish means delicious or exquisite, but *esquisito* in Portuguese means queer or peculiar.

Although the United States and Latin America have been living together in the same hemisphere for a long while they still do not understand each other. People in the United States cannot understand why the Latin American countries have not taken advantage of their resources and developed more rapidly, and why U.S.-style democracy has not prospered in many of them. Many Latin Americans, on the other hand, are suspicious of U.S. motives in Latin America, and they cannot understand why the United States with all its wealth is not doing more to develop Latin America. Although the United States is the world's largest source of aid, it ranks only seventh in terms of the percentage of GNP devoted to that purpose. It is outranked by Australia, Belgium, France, Germany, the Netherlands, and the United Kingdom.

The misunderstandings are vestiges of the historic pattern of relations between a large power and other states, a pattern which the contemporary international community no longer finds acceptable. Granted, it is difficult to eliminate friction between neighbors of disproportionate economic power, but we can minimize that friction if we regard economic disparity not as a cause for resentment or paternalism, but as evidence of the imperative need for closer cooperation. In spite of misunderstandings and misgivings, there is a growing awareness of the common interest of the nations of the Americas, and a desire for improved relations.

If historical friendship and geographical proximity alone do not justify U.S. support for Latin American development, there are two more obvious reasons, one political and one economic.

The political reason is that the United States wants to prevent violent revolution in Latin America, and the best way to do this is to help the countries win the quiet revolution.

The economic reason is that the United States needs additional trading partners. Trade is a two-way street. The greatest trade potential in the developing world lies in the Latin American countries.

In other words, cooperation with Latin America is not only vital for security but good for the economy. By helping to strengthen the Latin American countries the United States is also helping itself.

This is not to suggest that the unique relationship that links the United States and Latin America should limit commercial, cultural, and political relations with other countries or regions. However, United States cooperation in the development of Latin America should be a priority consideration for that country, based on considerations of enlightened self-interest rather than moral responsibility alone.

After discussions with 3,000 leaders in 20 Latin American countries in 1969, Governor Nelson Rockefeller's mission came to the conclusion that "National interest requires the United States to revive its special relationship with the nations of the hemisphere . . . with a new commitment; new forms, and new style."

The Rockefeller Report summed up, quite precisely, the feelings of a good many Latin Americans. It said, "The United States has talked about partnership, but it has not truly practiced it."

Why has the relationship between the United States and Latin America deteriorated? In no uncertain terms the Rockefeller Report suggests a number of reasons: the influence of narrow special interests, other foreign policy priorities, budgetary and balance-of-payments constraints, a burgeoning bureaucratic tangle, and a paternalistic attitude that assumed that the United States knew what was best for Latin America. Had these words been written by a Latin American, they might be dismissed as anti-U.S. propaganda. But they were published in the official report of a U.S. presidential mission, headed by one of the country's most distinguished authorities on Latin America, and they are helping to shape the Latin American policy of the Nixon Administration.

Preparation of the Rockefeller Report coincided with the

issuance of an extremely significant Latin American statement of the problems in inter-American economic relations: the Latin American Consensus of Viña del Mar. It was approved by the Special Committee for Latin American Coordination (CECLA) in May, 1969 and subsequently presented to President Nixon and to the Inter-American Economic and Social Council at its meeting in Port of Spain. This document reflects a growing tide of nationalism, regional cohesion, and solidarity in Latin America.

Shorn of its diplomatic amenities, the Consensus declared that the United States should make a greater effort to fulfill its obligations and commitments in the inter-American system.

The Consensus reiterated the Latin American countries' conviction that economic growth and social progress are basically their own responsibility, but that they need the support of the developed countries.

Among the major obstacles which the Consensus cited as a brake on Latin American economic growth are the conditions on trade and aid. In the area of trade, the main concern is with tariff and nontariff restrictions that impede access to the principal world markets under equitable or favorable conditions for Latin American raw, semi-processed, and manufactured products. In the area of aid, the Consensus cites the progressive deterioration of the volume, terms and conditions of international financing assistance.

Bearing in mind the recommendations of the Rockefeller Report and the Consensus of Viña del Mar, President Nixon outlined the framework of a new Latin American policy for the United States in an address to the Inter-American Press Association in October, 1969.

The address was a frank appraisal of some basic problems in inter-American relations. It contained a pledge to make a more positive contribution to the Latin American development efforts, without dictating the course of those efforts. It is particularly noteworthy that President Nixon decided to invite the Inter-American Committee on the Alliance for Progress to conduct a periodic review of U.S. economic policies as they affect the other nations of the hemisphere.

Mr. Nixon was right when he said that it is a time for action, not words. He was right if this time, as will hopefully be the case, these often-used words—that frequently hide a confession of impotence—do in fact result in forward-moving policies and measures. It is by its action that the United States will be judged, and Latin America has therefore understandably adopted a "wait and see"—yet hopeful—attitude with regard to the policy enunciated by Mr. Nixon. Latin Americans know that before the promise of increased cooperation can become a reality the President must convince the people and the Congress of the United States that Latin America's importance to the country warrants higher-priority treatment.

*The mixed reception—at times turbulent—accorded Vice President Nixon during his 1958 Latin American tour, opened the eyes of many Americans to the fact that all was not well in inter-American relations.*

In 12
Latin American countries
industrial production
rose by an average of nearly
50 percent in the sixties.
Canning plant in
Valencia, Venezuela.

# CHAPTER 4

# THE RECORD OF THE SIXTIES

Let us consider, for a moment, some of the principal trends in Latin America in the decade of the sixties.

Most important, perhaps, was the concerted effort to accelerate economic and social development and the determination to bring about changes in traditional institutions.

Economic growth continued during the decade, but at a slightly slower rate than in the fifties. The greater rates of population growth in most countries meant that per capita gross national product grew by about 1.7 percent annually in the sixties, as compared to 2.3 percent in the fifties.

Industrialization proceeded apace and, for the first time, manufacturing contributed a larger share of GNP than agriculture. In Latin America as a whole, manufacturing now accounts for one-fourth of the GNP, and agriculture one-fifth. Industrial production has consistently grown faster than the economy as a whole during the sixties. In 12 countries industrial production rose by an average of nearly 50 percent. In Panama and El Salvador production more than doubled; in Peru and Mexico it increased about two-thirds.

44

In the agricultural sector performance has been good, but not remarkable. Agricultural output increased substantially, keeping abreast of the population increase. Both the diversity of output and yields improved with more widespread use of fertilizer and improved technology, and some reforms in land tenure systems.

Between 1964 and 1968 government revenues increased 30 percent. Taxes as a percentage of GNP increased, reflecting the rising mobilization of domestic resources.

In the countries plagued by rampant inflation, the rate has been checked, especially in Argentina, Brazil, and Uruguay.

Despite some progress in diversification of exports, Latin America's share of world trade declined, and the prices of the region's exports rose more slowly than the prices of its imports. To import a tractor a country has to export twice as many bags of coffee or tons of ore as it did a few years ago.

Foreign private investment in Latin America continued to increase during the decade, particularly in manufacturing and trade rather than the extractive industries. U.S. direct investment increased by 43 percent between 1960 and 1967.

Movements for regional and subregional economic integration took shape, setting the stage for a future Latin American common market.

The literacy rate in Latin America rose from 67 percent in 1960 to an estimated 73 percent in 1970.* Enrollment in education at all levels rose at an average annual rate of 9.1 percent between 1960 and 1969, while the population in the 5-24 age bracket increased by 2.8 percent per year during the

*Regional averages in educational statistics hide great inter-country variations. The literacy rate ranges from a high of 98 percent in Barbados to a low of 24 percent in Haiti. School enrollment statistics of the various countries show similarly wide variations.

same period. This made it possible for the school enrollment ratio (number of students as a percentage of the population aged 5-24) to climb from 31 percent in 1960 to 45 percent in 1969,† (In North America, by way of comparison, the school enrollment ratio is about 67 percent.)

Considerable gains have also been recorded in health, particularly in the expansion of urban water-supply systems and sewerage. Latin American babies born in 1970 have a life expectancy 2.3 years greater than those born in 1960.

Apart from the quantifiable elements, there have been noteworthy institutional and administrative changes in Latin America. Economic growth in quantitative terms does not tell the full story of a nation's progress in the struggle for development. GNP does not tell how the national income is divided among the people, how public administration is being improved, or what is being done to achieve goals in education, health, housing, land reform, and employment. Some countries with high growth rates owe these mainly to fortuitous weather conditions or windfalls in export prices. On the other hand, some countries show lower growth rates because of the amount of resources being channeled into health or education, or because income is being redistributed more equitably and stabilization programs are in force. So we must consider not only the growth figures but the facts that modern management techniques are being introduced into the private and public sector, that economic development planning is becoming increasingly efficient and operational, and that institutions are being founded to mobilize savings, promote exports, stimulate

†In absolute terms, however, the enrollment increase of 23.4 million was almost matched by the population increase of 23.0 million, which means that the actual number of youth *not* enrolled in 1969—63.7 million—had declined by only about 400,000 since 1960.

industrialization, and strengthen agricultural extension. Also, the Catholic Church in many of the countries has become less of a defender of the status quo and more of an active champion of social justice. All of these institutions are having their effect on the framework of Latin American society.

In the Americas the First Development Decade of the United Nations essentially coincided with the Alliance for Progress, which was launched in 1961 with the Charter of Punta del Este, approved at a special ministerial-level meeting of the Inter-American Economic and Social Council of the OAS. The Alliance is the solemn commitment of the nations of this hemisphere to work together toward ambitious goals in economic and social development.

Unfortunately, the Alliance for Progress is misunderstood by generally well informed people throughout the Americas. In Latin America particularly, it is regarded as a bilateral U.S. program rather than a multilateral effort of all the member states of the OAS.

Throughout the author's visits to the member states in Latin America in 1968 he reaffirmed the true nature of the Alliance: that it is predominantly a Latin American program. When the late President John F. Kennedy defined the Alliance as "a vast cooperative effort, unparalleled in magnitude and nobility of purpose, to satisfy the basic needs of the American peoples for homes, work and land, health and schools," he was responding, in effect, to the views of several Latin American leaders, including former Brazilian President Juscelino Kubitschek, who had proposed an "Operation Pan America." Both the concept of the Alliance and the machinery for its coordination evolved within the Organization of American states.

The Alliance has three main components. The first, and most important, is the national effort within each country to overcome the obstacles to development. This effort includes education, tax reform, land reform, administrative reform. The governments want to encourage capital formation and infrastructure development within a climate of stability.

Multilateral action, through the inter-American system and the agencies of the United Nations family, is the second component of the Alliance. Preinvestment services of a multinational nature include evaluation of natural resources, training, research, and aid in planning. National efforts and requirements are reviewed multilaterally by the Inter-American Committee on the Alliance for Progress. The annual country reviews of CIAP, carried out in cooperation with national authorities and representatives of international lending agencies, facilitate multilateral coordination of aid and investment and give the countries leverage for their requests for external loans.

The third component of the Alliance is bilateral assistance. This includes not only the programs of the United States, but aid of various types of one Latin American country to another, and aid from states that are not members of the OAS. Several European countries, as well as Canada, Israel, and Japan, are now providing bilateral or multilateral aid to Latin America.

It is clear that the original timetable of the Charter of Punta del Este was overoptimistic. The same can be said of the worldwide goals of the First Development Decade, and the individual domestic goals of many of the developed countries. No amount of resources or determination could telescope into a decade the profound social and economic changes necessary to guarantee a decent standard of living for all.

The Charter of Punta del Este estimated that Latin America

would need a per capita economic growth rate of at least 2.5% per year in order to attain the goals of the Alliance. Due in part to rapid population growth, many of the countries have fallen short of this mark, as we have seen.

We often underestimate the extent of our advance. Progress is to be judged not only by how far we still are from the ambitious goals we have set for ourselves, but also by the distance we have traveled. The marginal advances that may be achieved from one year to the next in a wide range of fields—taxation, administrative reforms, planning, education, health, housing and others—often go unnoticed or are regarded as disappointing. The face of Latin America is changing rapidly and profoundly; and while this process inevitably brings with it new problems, problems resulting from change are preferable to those stemming from inertia.

During the decade of the Alliance the Latin American people, with perseverance and sacrifice, put forth tremendous efforts to meet their commitments. Seen in perspective, their achievements are significant:

- For the first time, national policy of each country has become development-oriented. The era of improvisation is fast disappearing.
- Coordinated efforts by the governments, supported by increasing complementary action by international organizations, were undertaken at both the preinvestment and investment stage.
- In spite of the difficulties, the governments accepted, committed themselves to, and began national programming for, development, with the establishment of specific priorities.
- A new generation of Latin American statesmen, econo-

mists, and technicians who speak a common language and have a firm grasp of the realities, the aspirations, and the possibilities of our countries has been trained.

- Physical integration has taken great strides with expanding highway networks, airways, river and sea routes, and modernization of telecommunications, in an era when satellites are on the verge of overcoming obstacles of geography and history.

- There has been spectacular progress in increasing school enrollment, especially in the primary grades, in many countries that had very low rates of enrollment.

- Large-scale social programs have improved housing, health, and education, to protect Latin America's most valuable asset, its human resources.

- In many areas local technicians together with multilateral and bilateral advisors have completed the studies indispensable for the evaluation of our resources and for sound planning. Our region is one of the most thoroughly studied in the world from the standpoint of economic potential. We are beginning to use computers for storage and retrieval of technical data related to development.

- Hundreds of prefeasibility projects have been defined. These are being financed by national capital, public and private, by national and international credit institutions, and by investors from many countries outside the Americas that are awakening to the opportunities opened by development in Latin America.

- For the first time, countries with chronic inflation have successfully undertaken stabilization policies. These continuing, austere policies, which require sacrifice by all sectors, can assure the gradual attainment of development in a climate of stability.

- Basic instruments and timetables for economic integration have been established. (See Chapter VII.)

These are some of the positive aspects of the Alliance. As indicated, the picture is not all bright. Realistic Latin Americans do not exaggerate the problems; neither do they ignore them, because recognition is the first step toward correction. Here are a few of the problems:

- There was insufficient technical tradition and expertise to fulfill the total program, and the image of the Alliance became distorted as a result of errors of definition and interpretation among the various countries.

- Many minimum goals were not achieved, as was the case in the United Nations Development Decade. This is basically a measure of hard reality of the world we live in, rather than the inadequacy or incapacity of the Latin American countries to achieve their goals.

- In many cases planners underestimated the importance of the national differences between the Latin American countries—in their levels of development, in their style of action, and in their sense of urgency.

- Impatience, external problems, and inevitable internal factors plagued many parts of the region with political instability that hampered constructive and systematic action.

- In spite of progress in its control, inflation continued to have detrimental economic and social effects.

- Capital outflow continued, and the growing burden of debt repayment weighed heavily on the Latin American economies.

- The growth of Latin America's export income has been unsatisfactory, owing in large measure to discriminatory obstacles on the part of the developed countries, and has adversely affected the availability of investment capital.

- Preferential tariffs were maintained by some of the former colonial systems, while the United Nations Conference on Trade and Development groped slowly toward solutions to the problem on a worldwide scale.

- In the region as a whole there was little progress in programs to ensure more equitable distribution of income and correction of serious social inequities.

- The brain drain continued, paradoxically drawing critically needed professionals from Latin America to the more developed countries.

- The effects of the cold war and political sabotage, as well as internal political tensions, affected the rhythm of development.

- Internal sectors with vested interests successfully resisted some governments' efforts to make badly needed reforms in the tax structure, public administration, and programs for agrarian reform and rural development.

- There were limitations on external credits offered by some countries, as well as disbursement delays and red tape.

In the chapters that follow we shall look more closely at progress and problems in a few of the areas that are of critical importance for the forward march of Latin American development.

The goal of the Alliance for Progress remains constant: a continent of peace and well-being, in which man can enjoy the full fruits of a free society. We know the enormous obstacles to development. We also know what must be done to overcome them.

A major economic objective of Latin America
in the seventies will be to
increase and diversify exports. Coffee loading
in port of Santos, Brazil.

# CHAPTER 5

# TRADE: A GIGANTIC BURDEN OF RESPONSIBILITY

An articulate young statesman of an underdeveloped country once wrote a sharp indictment of the trade and shipping policies of the developed countries: He said that the states of his region of the globe must unite against certain powers which are naturally bent on "fostering divisions among us, depriving us of an active commerce in our own bottoms, . . . monopolizing the profits of our trade, and clipping the wings by which we might soar to greatness."

The words sound like they might be those of a nationalistic Latin American accusing the United States of economic aggression, but they were actually written in 1787 in *The Federalist* by Alexander Hamilton. The underdeveloped nation in danger of having its wings clipped was the United States.

Today the shoe is on the other foot. History has been kind to the United States, bringing it to a position of unparalleled economic preeminence, in which its action—or inaction—has repercussions around the globe. This position places a gigantic burden of responsibility on the United States.

Today it is the Latin American nations and the other developing nations of the world that are calling upon the United States for greater trade liberalization, while at the same time seeking to assert their economic independence. On the basis of its own history, the United States should have no difficulty in understanding this position.

The continuing deterioration in Latin America's terms of trade is one of the major obstacles to the region's development. This grim economic reality spurs concerted efforts for diversification, but diversification takes time. Meanwhile, Latin America's share of world trade is actually shrinking.

Commodities remain the lifeblood of Latin American exports, despite a gradual change in the nature of the region's trade. In this connection, OAS studies show that tropical agricultural products and petroleum—the traditional principal items in Latin American commerce—are beginning to decline in relative importance. Temperate zone agricultural products and minerals show very slight percentage increases. The most striking advances are being made by nontraditional exports, including chemicals and refined minerals, though the amounts involved are still small. The OAS Inter-American Export Promotion Center in Bogota, Colombia, established in 1968, can encourage and develop this trend even further, provided, of course, external markets are liberalized.

We must restructure world trade so that the developing countries can increase their exports of manufactured as well as basic products, and in the process stimulate scientific and technological development. A decisive role could be played by the elimination of protective systems on the part of the industrialized countries and by the establishment of a more stable and remunerative system for the trade of the developing countries' products.

Roberto Campos of Brazil has pointed out the irony of the fact that the developing countries are expected to carry out politically difficult economic and social transformations, while developed countries consider it politically impossible to effect relatively minor changes in their trade structure. There is a double standard, whereby the developed countries consider their own competitive ability in world markets as "productive efficiency" while they regard the timid inroads in their markets of goods from developing countries as "market disruption."

There is nothing contradictory between the establishment of a commodity stabilization fund and continuing efforts to work out international commodity agreements for an ever-larger range of products. The negotiation of a new World Sugar Agreement is an encouraging step, even though it admittedly covers only about one-third of all sugar in world trade. The rest still moves through special preferential arrangements to Great Britain, the United States, the European Common Market, and the Soviet bloc.

Ideally, tariff preferences should be offered on a worldwide basis to all less developed countries by all developed countries on a non-reciprocal basis. Before considering a strictly regional system of trade preferences, we should exhaust every possibility of establishing a worldwide system of preferences that will not discriminate among developing countries or lead to the fragmentation of world commerce into more and more preferential blocs. We also should set a definite time limit on such efforts to create a worldwide tariff-preference arrangement vis-à-vis the developing world. Only if these efforts fail, within the time provided, should we begin to take a close look at what a regional system may offer.

We should make it very clear that extending trade preferences to less developed countries is not an act of international charity. If we are committed to creating a balanced world in which all nations have viable economies, there is no choice except to build the export capacity of the less developed countries through trade preferences.

Too often aid and trade are considered separately. This is a mistake. If the developed countries take positive steps to improve Latin America's foreign trade earnings, Latin America will need less aid, and will be able to purchase more from them. If aid is used effectively, it can promote increased domestic savings and export earnings in Latin America and thereby reduce the need for further concessionary financing. In the short run, however, cooperation in both trade and aid is necessary and desirable. The slogan "trade, not aid" is catchy, but it is unrealistic as long as protectionist sentiment prevails in the developed countries.

The problem is not only one of tariff preferences, involving mainly semiprocessed and manufactured products. Latin America faces the even more serious problem of restrictive quotas on many primary products, including cotton textiles, meat, and petroleum. Tariffs on such products are low or nonexistent in most cases, but the setting of arbitrary quotas restricts Latin America's earning possibilities on goods that are still of key importance in generating resources for development. New, energetic efforts to do away with these obstacles are an urgent necessity.

A major economic objective of Latin America in the seventies will be to penetrate foreign markets and increase and diversify exports. Unless the region can increase its exports by six or seven percent per year it cannot achieve the economic growth rates required for better living standards, reasonably full employment, and industrialization. Attainment of the desired growth in exports will require not only the concerted internal effort of the Latin American countries, but a more liberal and far-sighted attitude on the part of the world's major industrialized powers, particularly the United States and the European countries.

In summary, this is the type of cooperation in trade that the Latin American countries are seeking:

- Reduction or elimination of tariff and nontariff barriers to Latin American exports of all types.
- Establishment of a system of generalized trade preferences for manufactures and semimanufactures.
- Consultation prior to the imposition of measures affecting Latin America's trade.
- Establishment of national or inter-American systems of export credits.
- Elimination of discrimination against Latin American vessels and cooperation in the creation of Latin American merchant fleets.
- And, finally, stabilization of market fluctuations through commodity agreements, buffer stocks and supplementary financing.

In announcing his administration's Latin American policy in 1969, President Nixon offered to take four positive steps of benefit to Latin American trade: First, to lead a vigorous effort to reduce the nontariff barriers to trade maintained by nearly all industrialized countries against products of the developing countries. Second, to support increased technical and financial assistance to promote Latin American trade expansion. Third, to support the establishment, within the inter-American system, of regular procedures for advance consultation on trade matters. Fourth, to press in world trade forums for a liberal system of generalized tariff preferences for all developing countries.

This new approach of the United States, and the joint stand on trade matters that was assumed by the Latin American countries in the Consensus of Viña del Mar, made it possible for the Inter-American Economic and Social Council to establish a permanent Special Committee for Consultation and Negotiation in February, 1970.

In the area of trade, the ministerial-level Committee has the following functions:

- to hold consultations whenever a member of the inter-American system considers the United States has violated international stand-still commitments assumed by developed countries;
- to review restrictions adopted by the United States since November, 1963 which unfavorably affect imports of Latin American products;
- to conduct consultations between the United States and Latin America prior to adoption by the former of measures that might adversely affect imports from Latin America;
- to identify tariff and nontariff barriers to Latin American primary and manufactured products in the United States, with a view to eliminating those barriers;
- to review the system of unilateral or so-called voluntary

quotas set by the United States, so that in case of larger consumption or production shortfalls in the United States, the developing countries may get a larger share of the expanded market;

- to work together in international forums for the establishment of trade policies that will aid in the development of all developing nations, including a general system of nonreciprocal and nondiscriminatory preferences for products of the developing countries.

The establishment of the Special Committee is an important milestone in the history of international cooperation for development in the Americas, and augurs well for the strengthening of Latin America's trade posture in the seventies.

*Willys Automobile plant in Brazil. Latin America needs more joint ventures, in which foreign investors cooperate with local capital.*

# CHAPTER 6

# FOREIGN INVESTMENT

## ECONOMIC NATIONALISM

Foreign investment is a prime source of risk capital for Latin America. This is a type of financing not available from public sector sources, either foreign or domestic. Foreign investment brings with it a generous measure of management know-how and advanced technology—the accumulated techniques and skills of modern industry. Another advantage is the foreign investors' ready access to markets outside the country.

On the other hand, Latin American governments are also well aware of the shortcomings of private foreign investment. It is sometimes an expensive source of financing. It usually flows into the sectors or the particular countries where profit opportunities are best, often creating an uneven "bunching" of foreign investments. Moreover, private foreign investment is not likely to move into basic infrastructure projects.

It is also true that the foreign investor may not always identify his own interests with those of the country in which he operates. In the case of balance of payments problems back home, for example, he may have to repatriate profits in large doses, without reference to the balance of payments problems of the country in which he is located. He may be loath to compete with other foreign firms, or more specifically, with branches of his own firm in other countries.

Understandably, the foreign investor thinks first of profit potential and secondarily of development potential. But for many Latin Americans, the measure of the worth of foreign investment is precisely what it does for the economic and social development of their country. Under the new nationalism, only the foreign firm that is able to contribute to economic development and help promote healthy social progress is wanted. The firm that exploits a nation's resources without reference to the objectives of the country and the will of the people is unwelcome, not for being foreign, but for being insensitive to the local desire for reform and development.

Some time ago, Thomas J. Watson, Chairman of the Board of the International Business Machines Corporation, noted that the "United States is the largest off-shore investor in world history." If American branches and subsidiaries overseas were to form a nation, he said, "its gross national product would rank third in the world, following the United States and the Soviet Union." Direct private investment by American business in Latin America in 1970 comes to slightly more than $12 billion.

Present-day economic nationalism in Latin America, with its concern for national development and for social reform, is a far cry from xenophobic isolationism. Indeed, the new nationalism is distinguished by its regional spirit. For another of its goals is the establishment of a viable, regional Latin American economy, managed by Latin Americans, for the benefit of Latin Americans.

Unfortunately, many Latin Americans look upon all foreign business, and on American business in particular, as allied with the entrenched status quo. They see a panacea for most of their ills in the ending of economic domination by corporate giants. The best antidote for this type of resentment is effective cooperation by the foreign investor with Latin American nationalists who are working for development and reform.

There are a number of models on which effective cooperation by United States business in Latin America can be patterned.

More than 20 years ago Nelson Rockefeller created the International Basic Economy Corporation as a means of pioneering new ideas in Latin American investment. IBEC's main purpose was to stimulate private enterprise in certain areas deemed critical to national development. Many of these areas have been incorporated into national development plans, proving the essential far-sightedness of the Rockefeller approach.

Today, IBEC operates in such widely diverse areas as the development of supermarkets, banking, and the production of machinery for the chemical-processing industry. Its branches can be found from Brazil to Puerto Rico. It has never been a big money-maker, but it has always been long on social awareness. It makes less than one percent profit on its total assets and pays three times as much taxes in Latin America as in the United States.

If the low-profit example of IBEC doesn't commend itself to all American businessmen, there are countless firms that have made excellent profits while establishing solid economic and social ties in their host country. They buy all the goods they possibly can from local sources, hire local personnel and promote them to high executive positions.

Another model, perhaps even more pertinent to Latin America's mood today, is the ADELA Investment Company. The brainchild of Senator Jacob K. Javits of New York, ADELA is a multinational private investment company, founded on the principle that when capital comes from many countries, it loses its national identity. ADELA attracts investment not only from the United States, but from Latin American and European countries as well. And it channels its investments into projects that have a distinct multinational potential.

This is of crucial importance, for the future of Latin America lies in the economic integration movement and in the development of the private sector along multinational lines.

For the foreign investor, the message should be clear: the brightest opportunities lie in multinational joint ventures with Latin American participation.

As Latin America began to industrialize after World War II on the basis of national import substitution policies, tariffs were raised on certain imports, and free entry was granted to raw materials to be used by fledgling national industries. First, manufacturing plants in Latin America began to finish locally the semimanufactured products they obtained abroad, and today they undertake, in local plants, the complete manufacturing operation of a vast line of products. In the larger and more developed Latin American countries, local industries satisfy nearly all the domestic demand for consumer goods. Manufacturing subsidiaries in Latin America of U.S. companies, which at first were primarily distributors of United States products, have played a significant role in this development.

But possibilities for further growth along these lines are now limited. In many countries opportunities for import substitution in the case of consumer goods have been largely exhausted. The remaining investment opportunities are for the manufacture of the more complex products and of a few highly sophisticated and durable consumer goods. Frequently these cannot be produced efficiently and at a reasonable price within the confines of a single Latin American national economy because of the limitation of the market. Economic integration, thus, has become a precondition for satisfactory further growth.

The emergence of a larger, regional market offers great opportunities for an increased contribution by U.S. companies in connection with the Latin American development process, and will allow these foreign investors to enter many fields deemed important by the host countries or region. The manufacture, at the regional level, of more complex steel products, sophisticated production machinery, and petro-chemicals—including fertilizers and plastics—are but a few of the fields in which the activity of foreign companies could be extremely helpful.

It should be stressed, however, that the challenge thus offered to U.S. business in Latin America by integration is not principally related to the need for more capital. In fact, Latin American public opinion in the countries which have the most experience with direct foreign investment holds that furnishing capital itself is not the investor's most important function. If this were the only requirement, local businessmen might have done quite well by importing capital goods with credits repayable on the longest terms available, from institutions such as the Export-Import Bank. This alternative is open, but it is not enough. Further growth in Latin America, from here on, requires that new, more sophisticated technology and management know-how be allowed to spread through the entire economy, and that new local marketing and export opportunities be taken up by nationals. No foreign lender can provide this.

Foreign direct investment taking part in multinational companies, controlled from within Latin America, would be appropriate, in many instances, to fill the new needs of enlarged regional Latin American markets in a manner satisfactory to the host countries. Thanks to their connections in the United States and other developed countries, such multinational companies could draw on the capital, technology, and managerial know-how available in the United States and other developed countries. But their multinational character also would enable these companies to distribute their resources and functions throughout the Latin American area, so as to assure the most efficient operation and the greatest benefit to all countries where these companies operate, as well as to the foreign investors.

It is even more important that these multinational companies take on the character of joint ventures with nationals in the host countries. In many instances it should be the eventual goal to hand most of the ownership and operation over to local interests. Thus, the multinational corporations would be in an excellent position to disseminate technology and managerial know-how and create a nationwide climate favorable to modern, efficient business enterprise. The training of nationals within such multinational companies and the "demonstration effect" throughout the economy would lead to modernization of business in general and to further economic growth, thus widening the opportunities for both foreign and national firms. As local partners take on a more important role in running the firm and providing the capital for it, the transformation and accelerated expansion of the economy thereby engendered will assure foreign investors new and growing opportunities.

Most Latin American countries are pursuing policies and defining the rules of the game in a conscious and deliberate effort to attract investments from abroad, offering all the reasonable safeguards. While there has been nationalization, settlement on adequate compensation either has been reached or is in process. And while there may be further nationalization, especially in the extractive industries, these still constitute a very small proportion of the 16 to 18 billion dollars of direct private foreign investment in Latin America today. From the United States alone, gross additions to direct investment in Latin America still amount to more than 500 million dollars annually, an increasing proportion of which goes into manufacturing and commerce, much in the form of joint ventures or as minority holdings. These investments—geared to the local market—more and more are regarded not as foreign but as "naturalized" foreign enterprises, forming an integral part of the local business panorama, with major proportions of profits being reinvested locally. Little, if any, xenophobia or threat of take-overs faces those enterprises.

U.S. and other foreign investors in Latin America, in the past, have found it possible and profitable to adjust their activities to the changing requirements of their host country. The change from the pre-World War II situation, when direct foreign investment consisted largely of export-oriented enterprises—often in mining and petroleum—which were not greatly involved in the internal economy of their Latin American hosts, to that which now exists, when manufacturing for local consumption has become the most dynamic sector, has led to greatly enlarged benefits for the area. At the same time, forward-looking foreign investors in these new enterprises have found business just as profitable—if not more so—than before, while their relations with their host have improved, as a rule. Now a further, even greater, change is called for. Foreign companies which will help in making integration a reality by cooperating with local entrepreneurs in Latin America will find the results well worth their efforts.

Economic nationalism, if properly channeled, can drive this hemisphere to still greater efforts of self-discipline and self-help. It challenges the foreign investor and the national government to seek new means of accommodation and understanding.

*New
hydroelectric system
in El Salvador
provides power
for country's development.*

*Development assistance
for projects such as
this Colombian highway will
be channeled increasingly
through multilateral agencies
in the future.*

# CHAPTER 7

# DEVELOPMENT ASSISTANCE IS NOT A GIVE-AWAY

**E**ven presuming more favorable international policies on trade and private investment, there will still be a substantial need in the seventies for public external financial cooperation in Latin American development.

Specifically, the Latin American countries seek:

- Expansion of the volume of financial cooperation, so that they can achieve a net inflow of funds of reasonable magnitude, rather than net outflows as at present.

- An easing of lending conditions, with longer grace periods and lower interest rates, subsidized where necessary.

- Further untying of United States aid, so that it can be spent outside the Western Hemisphere, and more concerted efforts within the Organization for Economic Cooperation and Development to achieve an untying of credits by all industrialized countries.

- Cooperation in achieving a shift in policy of international financial institutions, to permit program or sectoral lending and the financing of local currency costs where needed.

The Latin American countries do not need more loans on hard terms. They are having enough trouble repaying hard loans already. Debt repayment eats up about one-third of their gross capital inflow. They need more of the type of genuine development assistance recommended by the Pearson Commission* loans at no more than two percent interest, with a grace period of from seven to 10 years and a maturity of between 25 and 40 years.

What part of Latin America's external development assistance should come from the United States? The General Secretariat of the Organization of American States, in a technical study presented to the Inter-American Economic and Social Council in 1969, suggested that the United States might furnish $1.1 billion to Latin America annually from 1970 through 1975. Although this is more than double the amount made available in recent years, it would not be unrealistic in terms of the commitment made by the United States at Punta del Este. The OAS proposal suggested that, of this $1.1 billion, $475 million be reserved for bilateral programs. The rest, $650 million, would be a nonreimbursable contribution to the Inter-American Development Bank. It would enable the Bank to mobilize more funds elsewhere, and increase its Latin American lending operations to $1.3 billion per year and soften the terms for those loans. Adoption by the United States of a policy of this nature

*The Commission on International Development, chaired by former Canadian Prime Minister Lester B. Pearson, made its report to the World Bank in September 1969. The complete report was published by Praeger under the title *Partners in Development.*

would be a tremendous boon to Latin American development. It would be a revolutionary breakthrough in inter-American relations.

The public in the United States, largely uninformed about the magnitude of the Latin self-help effort and the actual terms of U.S. assistance, views the latter as a give-away. The Latins, fully aware of their self-help effort and the fact that most U.S. aid is in the form of tied loans, question the sincerity of the U.S. commitment.

The expression "foreign aid" has the unfortunate and misleading connotation of a handout. Mutual assistance might be a happier term, for development assistance is certainly not a give-away. It is an investment in the future that pays daily dividends by stimulating the Latin American market for U.S. goods and services.

This is not to suggest that "aid" will buy friends. It won't. Latin America wants to be master of its own destiny and to make its presence felt in the world political arena. This is a logical exercise of responsible sovereignty, not an indication of a desire to flirt with communism or to renounce democratic values.

Since 1965 United States financial cooperation with Latin America has been shrinking, while the conditions on loans have become more onerous. Humiliating amendments have been made to the aid authorizations, inspired by internal political considerations. These have soured inter-American relations. The Hickenlooper Amendment,* a supposed deterrent against nationalization, is a case in point.

---

*The Hickenlooper Amendment provided for the withholding of U.S. financial assistance from countries that expropriate U.S. business interests without prompt and adequate compensation.

Much is heard in the United States, even in sophisticated circles, of the crushing burden of aid on the American tax-payer. Those who lament the burden usually overlook three basic facts:

First, only one-third of a cent of each taxpayer's dollar goes for economic cooperation with Latin America.

Second, around 80 percent of all official capital flows have been in the form of loans—not grants—and most of them are repayable in dollars. Fully half of the amount loaned during the sixties has already come back to the United States in the form of payments of principal and interest. Interest alone in the first seven years of the decade amounted to $734 million.

Third, of the loans made bilaterally by the United States Government as well as a large part of those extended by the Inter-American Development Bank in the late sixties, more than 90 cents of each dollar lent was spent in the United States, on United States goods and services. In other words, these were tied loans, which helped U.S. exporters but gave the borrowing countries little flexibility to shop around for the most favorable terms.

The fact of the matter is that the aid burden has rested largely on the receiver rather than the donor.

In terms of net capital flow, Latin America in some years actually aids the United States. In 1967 there was a net inflow of capital and service payments from Latin America to the United States amounting to some $500 million. Taking into account this fact, and the fact that United States aid was fully tied, it is clear that Latin America made a positive contribution to reducing the balance of payments deficit of the United States. Latin America, in effect, shared with the United States some of the sacrifices needed to safeguard the latter's external accounts.

In the early days of the Alliance for Progress, when miraculous progress in a decade was envisioned, the United States Congress was willing to back up the administration's commitment to make available $1 billion a year to aid Latin America's development. In recent years congressional enthusiasm has steadily waned, as is apparent from the shrinking appropriations. President Johnson's pleas for congressional support when he went to the summit meeting in Uruguay in 1967 were ignored. President Nixon has fared no better.

A former chief of the Agency for International Development once said that when AID asks for money to put out fires, it gets it; when it asks for money to prevent fires, it is accused of carrying on a give-away program.

The Chairman of the Inter-American Committee on the Alliance for Progress, Dr. Carlos Sanz de Santamaría, has said that Europe's rapid reconstruction after World War II would have been impossible if the United States Congress had attacked the Marshall Plan the way it is attacking the much more modest programs that seek to speed up development and progress in Latin America.

In the years following the war the United States actually did more to help its former enemies recover than it did to help its Latin American allies. It is interesting to speculate what Latin America would be like today if it had received a generous infusion of post-war U.S. aid. To be sure, Germany and Japan had a highly developed human and technical infrastructure which permitted rapid rehabilitation, despite the ravages of war, but could not aid of similar magnitude have at least helped Latin America to develop the infrastructure?

There have been some interesting editorial reactions of the press of the United States to the reduction of the foreign aid and Alliance for Progress appropriations by Congress. There are a few voices praising this action, claiming that "foreign aid has been marked by waste, futility, corruption, and wishful thinking"; that "aid should be in the nature of a reward"; and that "it's time for other nations to take on more of the load." Fortunately, these voices are in the minority. The overwhelming majority of editorials on the subject censure the congressional action. They call it "a national shame," "a black mark for the world's wealthiest nation," "national irresponsibility," "a major trauma for U.S. foreign policy," and "a sorry role."

It is often said that foreign aid is the most vulnerable part of a President's budget request because there is no voting constituency to come to its defense. It is clear that there is widespread public misunderstanding of the nature and role of international financial assistance.

Be that as it may, the cold, hard fact is that U.S. congressional appropriations for aid are shrinking every year, and there are few signs that the trend will be reversed in the seventies. It could be reversed only by a reordering of the global priorities of the United States and a firmer public conviction of the political and economic importance of Latin America's development to the United States.

In theory, if not in practice, Congress takes into account the recommendations of a multilateral mechanism for determining aid requirements: the Inter-American Committee on the Alliance for Progress, which was praised by the recent report of the Pearson Commission as a model regional development committee. CIAP has demonstrated that it can analyze each country's situation thoroughly and objectively, in cooperation with other international organizations. It makes recommendations regarding domestic effort and external cooperation without political strings.

Complementing the work of CIAP, a newer OAS organ, the Permanent Executive Committee of the Inter-American Council for Education, Science and Culture, will be responsible for reviewing and evaluating the efforts made by the member states in those fields.

Multilateralism deserves a much more substantial role in inter-American relations. The political pitfalls of bilateral economic cooperation have been all too clear in recent years. It is difficult for any powerful country to avoid charges of intervention when it decides unilaterally which countries should get aid, now much they should get, and under what conditions it should be granted.

In 1969, after the Latin American Consensus of Viña del Mar stressed the need to improve the volume, terms, and conditions of international financing assistance, the United States took three promising steps: it eliminated the ''additionality'' requirement, whereby a country could not reduce its imports from the United States if it wanted to receive a U.S. development loan; it untied loan dollars to Latin America, to the extent that they could be spent anywhere in the Latin American region; and it announced that it would review all other ''onerous conditions and restrictions'' on U.S. assistance loans with the objective of modifying them or eliminating them.

In addition, the United States proposed that a multilateral inter-American agency such as CIAP be given greater responsibility for development assistance decisions, to evolve an effective multilateral framework for bilateral assistance. The United States offered an initial contribution of $3,000,000 to strengthen the technical staff and field missions of CIAP.

The Special Committee for Consultation and Negotiation of the Inter-American Economic and Social Council, established in February, 1970, whose functions in the area of trade have previously been mentioned, was also requested to consider ways of improving development assistance procedures.

These developments may pave the way for more effective development assistance in the seventies.

*Tourism is*
*a major source*
*of revenue*
*for Uruguay.*
*Pocitos Beach, Montevideo.*

*Economic integration will eventually
broaden the market for all
Latin American industries.
Petroleum refinery in Venezuela.*

# CHAPTER 8

# THE ROAD TO ECONOMIC INTEGRATION

The amended Charter of the Organization of American States that entered into force in February, 1970 formally recognizes that the integration of the developing countries of the hemisphere is one of the objectives of the inter-American system. The treaty commits the member states to orient their efforts and take the necessary measures to accelerate the integration process, with a view to establishing a Latin American common market.

The commitment to integration is contained in the section of the Charter dealing with economic standards, but the desire for greater integration transcends economics. The qualifying adjective "economic" is significantly absent from the statement of the general goal of integration. Indeed, under the social standards of the amended Charter the member states recognize that, in order to facilitate the process of Latin American regional integration, it is necessary to harmonize the social legislation of the developing countries, and they agree to make the greatest efforts possible to achieve this goal. And in the educational, scientific, and cultural standards, the states recognize that regional integration programs should be strengthened by close ties in the fields of education, science, and culture.

The initial thrust of the integration movement, however, has been in the economic area.

The logic of the concept of economic integration is tellingly simple: in unity there is strength. Latin America as a whole can never be economically viable if it remains divided into separate compartments. We realize that by joining the compartments through economic integration we can accelerate productivity, use the region's resources more efficiently, and, what is very important, develop a stronger international bargaining position, particularly in trade policy.

We are fully conscious, however, of the obstacles to integration: the lack of a solid industrial base, the tradition of trading with the United States and Europe rather than with each other, inflation, the wide variation in level of industrialization of the countries within the region, the inadequacy of transportation and communications facilities, and political instability, to name but a few. The European Common Market did not face most of these obstacles.

The author had the privilege of serving as chairman of the working group of the United Nations Economic Commission for Latin American that drew up the preliminary plans for the region's economic integration in the late 1950's. These studies paved the way for the establishment of the Latin American Free Trade Association, which has come to encompass Mexico and all of the Latin republics of South America, and the Central

American Common Market, which links the five Central American countries. Both movements were launched in 1960.

The Central American Common Market has broad goals, similar to those of the European Economic Community. Its objectives are free trade among member countries, a common external tariff, and the coordination of fiscal, monetary, and investment policies. The Latin American Free Trade Association (LAFTA), has more limited aims, like those of the European Free Trade Association or Outer Seven. It seeks gradually to remove customs tariffs and other restrictions on mutual trade.

The methodology of the two movements also differs. The Central American Common Market accomplishes trade liberalization by across-the-board reductions, while LAFTA employs more cumbersome product-by-product negotiation.

Amazing the early skeptics who thought that the predominantly agricultural nations of Central America would have little to trade with one another, the Central American Common Market made tremendous progress in the sixties and became a source of encouragement to integration efforts elsewhere in Latin America. Duties have been eliminated on nearly all trade within the Central American region, which increased by 14 times between 1960 and 1969. During the same period the intraregional share of the Central American countries' total trade rose from six percent to 20 percent. Furthermore, the region has a common external tariff for about 80 percent of its imports. The Central American Bank for Integration has been successfully working to finance integration projects in this region and has been responsible for the development of a road network which has facilitated intra-Central American trade.

The 1969 conflict between El Salvador and Honduras temporarily interrupted the momentum of the Central American Common Market, but there is no doubt that by now the Central American integration movement is irreversible.

In the Latin American Free Trade Association, where the disparity between the level of development of the members is greater than it is in Central America, progress has been slower. Trade among the LAFTA countries slightly more than doubled during the past decade, and the intraregional share of their total world trade increased from six percent to 10 percent. Although the countries have granted a substantial number of tariff concessions in the national lists—more than 11,000— these involved for the most part products which the countries do not yet produce. Furthermore, it is estimated that only 30 percent of the concessions are utilized. With the easy concessions granted, negotiations have bogged down. The timetable for concessions on the common list, which is binding on all countries, had to be delayed. In December, 1969 it was decided that the Free Trade Zone, originally supposed to be in effect by 1973, would have to wait until 1980.

Within LAFTA, five countries—Bolivia, Chile, Colombia, Ecuador, and Peru—have embarked on more rapid and more comprehensive economic integration, seeking to develop not only a free trade area but an economic community, with joint industrial programming, and harmonization of economic and social policies. The author represented the President of Ecuador at the Bogotá meeting in 1966 which led to the establishment of this subregional group. The treaty of Cartagena or Andean Pact, in force since December, 1969, commits the countries to automatic tariff reductions and a common external tariff by 1980.

As relatively less-developed countries, Bolivia and Ecuador will have until 1985 to bring their tariffs in line with the rest of the sub-group. Venezuela participated in the planning for the Andean Pact but has not yet signed it. The Pact will remain open for Venezuela's signature until the end of 1970. To finance multinational projects in support of subregional integration, the countries have established the Andean Development Corporation, with initial authorized capital of $100,000,000.

Another subregional economic integration movement in the Americas, not yet related to LAFTA or the Central American Common Market, is the Caribbean Free Trade Association (CARIFTA). Eleven Commonwealth nations and territories are members of CARIFTA, including Barbados, Jamaica, Trinidad and Tobago, which also belong to the OAS. As its name implies, its objective is limited to the establishment of a trade area rather than the development of a common market with a common external tariff. Trade barriers are to be progressively lowered among the members of the Association so that free trade in most products is achieved within five years for the relatively more developed members and within ten years for the less-developed members.

To promote regional-scale industrialization in the Caribbean, the CARIFTA members, joined by Canada and Great Britain, established the Caribbean Development Bank. Formally launched in January, 1970, the Bank has an initial capitalization of $50,000,000.

In the River Plate region of South America a multinational project of great potential has begun. In April, 1969 Argentina, Bolivia, Brazil, Paraguay, and Uruguay signed a treaty establishing an Intergovernmental Coordinating Committee to develop bilateral and multilateral infrastructure projects within the region. The OAS is assisting with natural-resource surveys, which are the prerequisite for specific development projects.

The big question in the minds of many Latin American leaders is how fast it will be possible to move ahead in the seventies toward the convergence of the various existing economic integration movements. The American Chiefs of State, meeting in Punta del Este, Uruguay in 1967, called for the gradual merger of the existing systems, so that a Latin American common market would be substantially in operation by 1985. At present, it would seem that the target is overly optimistic. The sense of urgency about integration is far from uniform, and some of the larger countries are more concerned with integrating their domestic markets first.

A first meeting of officials of LAFTA and the Central American Common Market to discuss the problems of meshing the two movements was held in 1968, but it made little progress and the meeting scheduled for 1969 was postponed. The inte gration groups are not yet ready for merging.

With the exception of the Andean Group, there has been an apparent decline in emphasis on the integration movement since the 1967 Declaration of the Presidents of America, which was signed at the summit meeting in Punta del Este, Uruguay. This coincides with renewed effort on the part of the Latin American countries to obtain a system of generalized preferences from the industrialized countries, especially for their manufactured and semimanufactured products.

Latin American countries are more united in defense of their trade interests than ever before, as evidenced by the joint position taken in the Consensus of Vina del Mar, but even with this new cohesiveness, and even if they are successful in obtaining full support from the United States, it is unrealistic to expect spectacular and rapid changes in world trade policies. It will be a long, slow process. This is all the more reason why it is in the Latin American countries' interest to concentrate on expanding trade with each other, a process which does not depend on decisions of the industrialized countries.

It would be a mistake to try to solve Latin America's trade problems with the industrial countries without at the same time attacking the problems that restrict trade within the region.

The Latin American countries must open up new markets within the area for their products, especially for manufactured and semimanufactured products which are not always competitive with those of the developed countries. The economies of scale that are possible in a broader regional market can make Latin American industries more competitive. If the relatively less-developed countries of Latin America are to get their share of the benefits of economic integration, trade policy must be coordinated with a regional investment policy and regional planning.

One factor which should facilitate regional planning and regional investment policies in the seventies is the current trend toward use of multilateral channels for external financial assistance. The Inter-American Committee on the Alliance for Progress (CIAP), an OAS organ, may be expected to have an important role in this process of multilateralization in the Latin American area. CIAP has already sponsored meetings in Central America with Common Market officials and representatives of international financial institutions to discuss the development of several multilateral projects in that region. This type of co-operation may be extended to the Andean Group, CARIFTA, and the River Plate Coordinating Committee, adding a broader dimension to regional planning and preparing the ground for eventual convergence of the movements.

Integration is just one of the many weapons that can be brought to bear in the struggle for economic and social development. It must be regarded as one aspect of an overall strategy of regional cooperation, planning, and coordination. It is not a panacea or an end in itself. And it is most assuredly a long-term process that may take decades to complete, because of the social, political, and economic obstacles that lie in its path. Progress will inevitably be uneven. The important point is that the process is under way, and that it is irreversible.

Jamaican plant produces
cement for export throughout
the Caribbean. Jamaica
is a member of the Caribbean
Free Trade Association.

# CHAPTER 9

# THE URBAN DILEMMA

The plight of the cities is one of the very few problems which plague the developed and underdeveloped countries alike. The United States, with a vibrant, dynamic economy, is confronted with sickness and decay in its cities. In Latin America, the slum problem is passing from bad to worse and we lack the capital to cope with it.

Yesterday, the *campesino* was bound to the land he worked and to the village in which he was born. Today, he is free, physically and psychologically. He is mobile for the first time in memory. And therein lies part of our problem.

The current urban dilemma is a combination of unchecked, unplanned growth and the seeming inability of our institutions to cope with it. We can not stop the flow of migration to our cities, nor can we provide for the migrants when they arrive.

What is behind this problem? For decades, it has been more than tradition—it has been almost a declaration of faith—that

*Latin America's urban population will double in the next fifteen years. Downtown São Paulo, Brazil.*

urban policy had little or no relation to national and regional development plans. The economic planners were too long content to measure their success in increments to per capita income—as if an average increase of two dollars a year among all the wage earners of the country would be of much comfort to an unemployed laborer in a shanty.

City administrations, for their part, have fought any encroachment on their jurisdiction by national development authorities. But in the past decade, urban problems have mushroomed, and all of us—politicians and planners, economists and sociologists, pastors and pundits—are now ready to admit that urban problems can be solved only within the larger context of national development and national change.

It is time to say bluntly that Latin America cannot hope to achieve the economic development and the social well-being it seeks unless it arrests the decay of its cities. It is time to make urban policy an integral part of development planning. It is time to break down the walls of varied scientific disciplines and seek a coordinated, multilevel approach to the urban dilemma.

Current rates of urban growth will not decline within our generation. The prospect is that they will continue to rise even more rapidly in the foreseeable future. Latin America's urban population increased by 50 percent in the past 15 years. In the next 15 years it will double.

It has frequently been pointed out that Latin America has the highest rate of population increase of any major region of the world. We are adding to our population at the rate of roughly three percent per year. But consider: we are adding to our *urban* population at a rate of from five to seven percent per year. There is scarcely a major city in Latin America which will not have to provide for twice its present population by 1980. Today, slightly more than half of all our people live in cities. By the year 2000 almost three-quarters will be urbanites.

The cause of this startling growth is, of course, migration from rural to urban areas. Fertility rates in the city are no higher than those in the countryside. In most cases, they are slightly lower. But each year thousands upon thousands of migrants leave the farms and villages to pour into big cities of each of our countries.

What kind of man is the migrant? He is not content with his lot. He wants something better for himself and for his family. He will not be tied down by homesickness, uncertainty of the future, or faltering courage. He packs what few belongings he has, and sets off with his family for the city, where he has heard there are marvelous opportunities for a man willing to work to get ahead.

When the migrant arrives, he does indeed find many of the marvelous things he had heard about. There may be schools for his children, close enough to walk to. There are drugstores at each corner, and doctors and clinics. There are department stores, theaters, and busses. So many exciting things to do and so many new neighbors to talk to!

If he is very, very lucky, there may even be a job. Too often, there is none. Lacking elementary education—he is probably illiterate—lacking all but basic farm skills—and lacking a patrón* in government to turn to, the migrant drifts into that ever-increasing wedge of urban population that sociologists call "marginal." For these are the people who inhabit the

---

*Under the *patrón* pattern in Latin American rural culture, landowners are responsible for the well being of workers on their estates, and the workers can turn to them for medical care and other assistance.

*callampas,* the *favelas,* the *tugurios,* the *barriadas*—call them what you will—of our cities. Their number is rising at an alarming rate—between 10 and 15 percent a year. In some relatively important Latin American cities, they have already come to constitute a majority of the population.

These are the slum dwellers, the denizens of the ghetto. Their plight sums up the sickness of all our cities. They are men who once made their way in the world by plowing the land, chopping cane, or picking coffee beans. They came to the cities and the cities failed to answer their dreams of a better life. In their misery lies the possibility for untold mischief: in cities all over this hemisphere, the plight of the ghetto dwellers is already being exploited for disruptive ends by demagogues.

Our countries must be prepared to pay a high price in what are called "social services" to improve these ghettos. Indeed, such things as education, health, public housing, fresh water, sewerage, and, lately, fresh air are now recognized as social rights, as the necessary conditions to minimal human existence, and governments must make every effort to provide them to all. To some extent, their existence may encourage the migrant to remain in the city, even under otherwise adverse circumstances.

Take education. There has been an enormous increase in school enrollment at all levels since the beginning of the Alliance for Progress. As a matter of fact, one out of four Latin Americans is presently involved in the educational process at some level.

In sanitation, the goal of the Alliance for Progress was to provide potable water and sewerage systems to 70 percent of the urban population and 50 percent of the rural population by 1971. At this time it seems likely that the target for potable water will be met in the cities, but not in rural areas. The sewerage target will not be met in either case.

The prospects for satisfying the enormous needs of this hemisphere for housing are even dimmer. It is calculated that one million housing units a year must be built in Latin America's urban areas to begin to overcome the housing gap. By 1975, the cities will require 1.8 million units a year and Latin America overall will need 2.6 million units per year. The cost by the end of this century would amount to $50 billion. The present rate of licensed housing starts—for those who want to compare performance with need—is only 400,000 units per year, of which barely 100,000 are in the low income category. Obviously, people do live somewhere, and the difference between need and starts is made up by the shacks that dot the landscape of our cities.

It is apparent that urbanization is taking place in Latin America without the necessary investments in urban infrastructure and adequate planning. Aside from housing itself, gaps in water supplies, gas, electricity, drainage, transportation, schools and hospitals are growing every year.

It has been estimated that between 1968 and 1980 no less than 80 billion dollars should be invested in the countries of South America just to house the additional population and provide it with services. This estimate does not overcome the existing deficits in housing and services.

Despite commendable efforts, such as the establishment of the Social Progress Trust Fund within the Inter-American Development Bank, social spending has yet to come into its own. As a matter of fact, as national outlays have risen in recent years—educational budgets are the best example—soft money available from international lending institutions has been tapering off. With continuing cutbacks in the amounts of money appropriated for development by the industrialized countries, the likelihood is even greater that social projects—and by implication, the cities—will be the primary victims.

As the regional organization of the hemisphere, the Organization of American States has become increasingly concerned with the problems of urbanization. It has undertaken several action and research programs. CIAP analyzes data on urbanization, labor affairs, housing, and health in its annual reviews of the economic progress achieved by member states of the Alliance.

Within the General Secretariat of the OAS, a population program is endeavoring to advise member states on the intimate relationship between population and development. The implications for urbanization studies are obvious. Similar programs are under way in the area of labor affairs and development of cooperatives. A pioneering program in the restoration of historic urban areas has been undertaken in Quito, Ecuador, in cooperation with the OAS General Secretariat. One interesting side result of such restoration will be the promotion of tourism, with its attendant economic benefits.

We are, of course, concerned generally with the whole question of urban housing decay. We have under consideration now a study of the economic impact of housing programs on the development effort, an area in which economists and sociologists have not always been in agreement.

We are also trying to bring a measure of coordination to the training of urban planners and developers. There are a number of training centers in Latin America, including those operated by the OAS in Colombia and Peru.

But no one international organization, nor any single government agency has the answer to the massive problems that spell life—and perhaps death—for our cities. In size and in nature, the task ahead of us is without parallel.

We must begin immediately to weave urban strategy into the fabric of development. We have ignored it, compartmentalized it, distorted it for too long. The absence of urban policy in our overall planning has been one of the great shortcomings of the program.

At the international level, organizations like the OAS must devote more resources and attention to training and research activities in urban affairs. International lending agencies, such as the Inter-American Development Bank, must seek to divert more funds to housing, schools and transportation. In this connection the agencies must begin to give thought to making loans for certain current expenditures in the social field—maintenance of educational systems, for instance—for these are major budget items for many of our countries. Finally, the lending agencies should study ways to relieve the enormous and growing debt burden of Latin nations. Various different schemes have been proposed, but the important thing to remember is that Alliance countries are now spending one-third of all the money they receive as financial assistance on debt service. It is difficult, if not impossible, to fund the necessary social development programs under these circumstances.

At the national level, the first priority is to develop a strategy for population distribution. Such a strategy would include policies on industrial distribution, size of secondary and tertiary cities, transportation and communication—in short, integrated planning on urban-rural balance.

To paraphrase the song, maybe you can't keep 'em down on the farm, but you can make it attractive for them to live and work in smaller towns and cities. By so doing, you may even keep them in agricultural activities, given the proper developmental mix. But the pressures that have produced one or two large cities in most countries must give way to rational decisions about population balance. The proper incentives can be created to make small-town and small-city life quite attractive.

Since colonial times most Latin American municipalities have occupied a weak position vis-à-vis strong central governments. With few exceptions, cities and provinces have had extremely limited powers. This situation is gradually changing, however, and problems of conflicting and overlapping jurisdictions are becoming more widespread. To deal effectively with our cities' problems we need more joint regional authorities, which encompass all political jurisdictions with an interest in a particular area.

Such regional authorities will not only be better equipped to manage the development programs of far-flung metropolitan areas; they will also be more likely to take the long view on such matters as industrial location. There are many different interests in the establishment of a factory, not the least of which may be the unemployment rate in the immediate vicinity of the plant.

The really crucial task at the local level—and the one that has been most neglected—is the development of human resources.

The existence of large numbers of marginal workers in urban ghettos is an indication that our educational systems have been out of touch with the manpower needs of society. The man in the ghetto is capable of learning new skills. Indeed, he is anxious to do so. Up to now, those in government have not been anxious enough to give him the opportunity.

Training for the "new technology" is one aspect. Training for membership in the new urban society is another and equally important part. Anyone who has studied Latin American slums is struck by the high degree of implicit social order in an otherwise chaotic existence. There is a power structure; there are even "unofficial officials." Clubs and social organizations spontaneously emerge. These are not aimless, formless communities. If nothing else, they have the common experience of poverty to bind them together.

Governments must learn to communicate with these people. Untold havoc has been wreaked in planning offices where the voice of humanity is never heard, where there is no awareness of real human beings, but only of large numbers of abstract citizens. Let the voice of the people invade the planning offices and the city council chambers. For if we truly believe in democracy, we must let it work—and work on us—at all levels from the lowest to the highest.

*1970 Nobel Peace Prize
winner Norman Borlaug
(wearing hat) shows
new wheat varieties to members
of the Board of Directors
of the International Center
for the Improvement of
Corn and Wheat,
including the author (second
from left).*

# CHAPTER 10

# THE FARM PROBLEM AND THE GREEN REVOLUTION

**L**atin America's farm problems differ from those of the United States in both type and degree. In the United States a relatively small rural population produces so much that storage of the surplus becomes a major economic burden. Yet, by cutting back on production of some items, the farmers can maintain a decent standard of living. In Latin America there is a relatively large rural population which produces too little, and there is widespread rural poverty.

In the United States, one farmer can raise enough food to feed twenty urban workers and feed them well. In Latin America, one farmer feeds only one or two of his city cousins, and there is widespread malnutrition. The Latin American countries must often use scarce foreign exchange to import foodstuffs that could be produced locally. It has been estimated that, just to meet its own needs, Latin America would have to produce 50 percent more carbohydrates and 100 percent more protein by 1980. However, the prospects for increased production in some of the basic crops are very bright indeed.

For example, the International Maize and Wheat Improvement Center (CIMMYT) is revolutionizing agriculture through the introduction of improved high-yield, disease-resistant, fertilizer-responsive varieties of wheat and corn. CIMMYT is a research and educational institution in Mexico governed by an international board of directors of which the author has been a member since 1966. It has a staff of skilled scientists of various disciplines and nationalities.

The CIMMYT-Mexico dwarf wheats have had a striking impact in Mexico, India, Pakistan, and Turkey and show great possibilities for Latin America. In Mexico alone, in an area of about 1,500,000 acres, average yields have doubled during the past decade. These varieties have suddenly made wheat production highly profitable for both farmers and the country. Production increase has stimulated the demand for fertilizers, pesticides, and farm machinery and, consequently, brought about a greater demand for better housing, more and better schools, more warehouses, more trucks, better roads and more electricity. All of this means a better life for many people.

Possibilities of maize improvement are even more spectacular, as a result not only of the introduction of high-yield, disease-resistant and broadly adapted varieties, but also of the introduction of commercial varieties with a greatly increased lysine content of the grain, which makes it 100 percent more nutritive. There are many people throughout Latin America who subsist on a low-protein diet of almost nothing but corn. This brings about all sorts of problems in malnutrition, particularly in the case of growing children. It used to be thought that the only way to correct this situation was to change their diets by introducing food of a higher protein value. You can just imagine the problem of changing eating habits of people that have not varied for centuries. Now, with the new high protein corn, this will not be necessary, because the new corn will supply the protein requirements.

Of course this great "green revolution" cannot transform things overnight. Many fundamental improvements and changes will have to take place before a majority of the rural people take advantage of these great scientific achievements which are now out of the laboratory, beyond the experimental plot, and being produced commercially.

One major problem is the insufficient use of fertilizers and pesticides in much of Latin America. The Food and Agriculture Organization has estimated that Latin America's food production could be increased by 20 percent with the use of pesticides, and that it could be doubled by adequate applications of fertilizer.

Lack of mechanization is another problem. Some countries have only one tractor for each 3,000 acres of cultivated land.

But tractors and fertilizer cost money, which is something that the small farmer lacks. There are still too few sources of credit open to him. Many of the farmers who practice the slash-and-burn ways of their ancestors do so not from ignorance but from lack of the initial capital needed for a new type of farming.

In many cases, however, it is the improper use of existing resources that is responsible for low productivity. Irrigation methods are a case in point. It has been estimated that throughout Latin America half or more of the water available for irrigation is wasted. A study by the Inter-American Committee for Agricultural Development in one large sugarcane growing region, where fields were being irrigated for two months each year, showed that the cane actually needed six to nine months of irrigation for full growth. The cost of the additional irrigation would be negligible.

In other words, lack of knowledge is as great a bottleneck to rural progress as lack of credit. Technological progress in the laboratory and research center and discoveries such as high-lysine corn are worthless if they cannot be translated into practice on the farm through an effective agricultural extension program.

On the ranches, lack of pasture-improvement programs, poor sanitation, and improper management often give rise to poorly fed cows, with irregular and far-spaced calving periods, which provides inadequate dairy production to meet the minimum per capita requirements of the population.

Another serious cause of underutilization of land and human resources in rural Latin America is the traditional system of land tenure. In much of Latin America the size of the landholdings tends toward extremes: a few estates of gigantic proportions—the *latifundios*—and a great number of farms that are too small to be economically self-supporting—the *minifundios*.

The owner of the *latifundio*, who has plenty of cheap labor and unexploited land, too often enjoys a life of ease in the city without overly concerning himself with technological advances which would increase the productivity of his land.

Large farms take up roughly three times as much of the farm area in Latin America as they do in the United States.

Despite the trend toward larger farms in the United States, most of them are small by Latin American standards. In the United States 3.7 percent of the farms occupy 49.2 percent of the country's farm area. But in Argentina, for example, 1.3 percent of the farms occupy 47 percent of the farm area. In Brazil, one percent of the farms occupy 44 percent of the farm area. And in Mexico, even after fifty years of agrarian reform, 1.6 percent of the farms occupy 78 percent of the total farm area.

This is not to imply that large farms are inherently bad; but they are bad if they are unproductive.

Other obstacles to increased productivity are the physical and cultural conditions of the rural labor force. Since three rural families out of four do not have a safe water supply, intestinal diseases naturally sap their strength. Doctors and clinics are often inaccessible. In most countries the intake of calories and proteins is below established international minimum levels. Ignorance and superstition are other brakes on progress. In several countries two-thirds of the rural population is illiterate. These problems are being slowly overcome, but they will take time.

In the meantime, millions of farm workers, unable to achieve a decent standard of living in the country, are moving to the city. As noted above, all too often they cannot find a job there either. Industrial expansion has been considerable, but it has not been able to create jobs fast enough to absorb the growing numbers of urban unemployed.

Although the rural labor force in Latin America continues to grow, its relative percentage in the national labor force is declining. In 1950, 60 percent of the region's total labor force was engaged in agriculture. Today, only 42 percent is still on the farm. Most of the shift has not gone into manufacturing but into services. This trend will undoubtedly continue, so it is imperative that agricultural productivity be increased to feed the growing urban population, and that rural incomes be raised to create effective markets for domestic industries. One of the major obstacles to industrialization in Latin America is the shallowness of the rural market, where the majority of the people have little to spend on the products of industry.

What is being done, and what must be done, to solve these problems? The key objectives are to create new jobs in agriculture and to ensure that the existing jobs are more productive. The three principal techniques for achieving these objectives are diversification, modernization, and conservation.

By diversification, we mean that, in addition to traditional sources of revenue such as coffee and bananas, the countries must produce new lines of raw, semiprocessed, and processed agricultural products for internal consumption.

By modernization, we mean the discarding of traditional farming practices and introduction of more efficient methods. Rapid and complete mechanization is not the answer in many areas, however, because it would aggravate the problem of rural unemployment. Mechanization should be introduced gradually and with care.

By conservation, we mean the reforestation and reclamation activities that are necessary to preserve and enrich the precious resource that is the soil. In countries where virgin land is plentiful there is a tendency to underestimate the importance of conservation, and this, of course, is a mistake.

If diversification, modernization, and conservation are to

be carried out on a meaningful scale, national agrarian development programs must make four things available to the farmer: land, technical assistance, credit, and markets. All four are indispensable for rural development. Legislation in most of the countries now recognizes the social function of property and the right of the state to expropriate property when the interest of society requires it. This public expropriation should not be confused with illegal seizures by extremist groups. Public expropriation provides for adequate compensation, with respect for due process of law. It is simply a way of attacking a semi-feudal system of land tenure. Mexico, Bolivia, and Venezuela have made the greatest progress in carrying out land distribution and land-resettlement programs. In most of the other countries, however, the programs are still in their early stages.

Establishment of producers cooperatives is one excellent way for small farmers to pool their resources of land and make them economically viable. For example, in Ecuador two rice cooperatives with 88 member families have bought nearly 2,000 acres of land on the installment plan and secured credit to buy improved seed, fertilizer, tools, irrigation pumps and a tractor. The families are experiencing a marked improvement in their standard of living.

For maximum effectiveness, technical assistance and credit should go hand in hand and should reach the small farmer. The Brazilian Rural Credit Association (ABCAR) is one of the typical agencies in Latin America created to perform both functions, and within the limits of its resources it has been successful. We recognize that substantial contributions in the form of technical assistance and credit for rural Latin America have been made by the United States Government, U.S. private foundations, and international organizations.

One unfortunate byproduct of this aid has been the tendency among Latin American agricultural planners to feel that foreign experts can offer better solutions than domestic experts. This is not always so. Qualified Latin American agronomists, who know their countries' problems well and could make a decisive contribution to solving them, often don't get the chance to try. They are paradoxically forced to go abroad if they wish to put their talents to work. This waste of human resources should be stopped, by making provision for use of domestic expertise wherever possible.

In their efforts to concentrate on the problems of land, technical assistance, and credit, many of the Latin American governments have paid insufficient attention to the question of markets. Market improvement, with the construction of cold-storage facilities, warehouses, wholesale markets, and the roads to reach them must be an integral part of agricultural development. It does a farmer no good to produce more if he cannot sell it before it spoils.

I would like to emphasize the importance of tax policy as a means for achieving the objectives of balanced agricultural development. Tax reductions can encourage investments that will increase agricultural productivity. At the same time, increased taxation of idle land can force it into production. Few Latin American countries have made full use of this powerful tool.

In short, the pressing problems of agricultural development in Latin America must be attacked simultaneously on many fronts to provide a firm foundation for continued economic and social progress.

*In Argentina,*
*1.3 percent of the farms*
*occupy 47 percent of the farm area.*
*Sheep ranch in southern Argentina.*

*Bolivian farm workers
take a course in
democratic union principles
high on the Andean altiplano.*

# CHAPTER II

# ESCAPE ROUTES FROM DESPAIR

At least 25 percent of the Latin American labor force was unemployed or underemployed in 1960 and the percentage today is believed to be even higher. The overwhelming proportion of workers in the existing labor force have no really marketable skills, and hundreds of thousands of young people are pouring into the labor market each year with preparation for only the most menial kind of work, at a time when technological change calls for increasingly skilled workers. This poses serious challenges for the seventies.

Great disparities in the distribution of income can put a brake on economic development. They mean inadequate markets, inefficiently small-scale operations, idle productive capacity, and a loss of incentive to invest. When higher wages help create a better balance between the power to produce and the power to consume, they encourage development. Unions which perform their traditional basic function of seeking a fair share of the benefits of economic progress for their members, with due regard for the need to maintain a proper balance between investment and consumption, are serving not only their members' interest but the national interest as well.

Responsible performance of the unions' traditional role will do much to meet the crying need for greater productivity in Latin America. Better wages enable workers to obtain adequate diets and decent housing; an orderly grievance procedure eliminates the inclination to resolve differences over work rules, contract interpretation, or disciplinary action by resort to work stoppages; and adequate protection against layoffs reduces the fear of changes in production methods. The higher morale resulting from a healthy labor-management relationship makes significant gains in productivity possible. It leaves little justification or incentive for restrictions on output or the withholding of maximum effort in any other form—a practice which is especially damaging in countries in which such vast numbers of people live so close to the margin of subsistence.

Besides the traditional role, there are other important ways in which unions can and should contribute to the development process.

As a representative of a significant segment of the population, trade unions have a part to play in drawing up and carrying out national development plans. Communication and consultation with trade unions is necessary to enlist labor's active enthusiasm for development programs. Labor can give greater social content to the plans, to ensure that they pursue the goal of maximum possible employment, that they focus on the need to raise the standards of living of the poverty-stricken, and that they strive, in general, to benefit the entire community, and not just a powerful minority.

Trade-union participation in development planning can inject a greater sense of realism into the planning process. "Planners too," as Raúl Prebisch* has said, "are fallible. Only too often we study the past and plan for the future, while knowing nothing about the present."

Union participation in development planning is also an eye-opener for labor. As unions come to participate more actively, their leaders are compelled to become better informed about national problems, they establish their own research departments or obtain help from other professional sources, and they come to take a broader view and reconcile their objectives with the national interest.

Another area, outside of their traditional field of action, in which unions can make an important contribution to development is education, particularly vocational education. The proportion of skilled persons among production workers in the labor force in Latin America in 1965 was extremely low; less than 10 percent were classified as artisans and skilled operators. The overwhelming proportion has no really marketable skills and only a small number (approximately six percent) is regarded as semiskilled. Estimates of the need for skilled production workers in 1980 indicate that the proportions should rise from the present 10 percent to a minimum of 15 percent. This would require approximately a tripling of the present number of skilled production workers.

The problem is one of staggering proportions and unions can and must play a part in alleviating it. They are already

*Raúl Prebisch is the former Executive Secretary of the United Nations Economic Commission for Latin America and former Secretary General of the United Nations Conference on Trade and Development.

doing so in a number of cases. There are instances of unions operating vocational training institutions either on their own or jointly with employers and government. In some cases unions are assuming responsibility for primary education, undertaking literacy campaigns and running nurseries. These efforts may appear modest in light of the enormous needs, but they are making a contribution to development; they are increasing national productivity, and they are opening up "escape routes from despair" for many prospective entrants into the labor force.

Unions have other vital functions in the development process: They can contribute to the operation and expansion of health and social security programs, which make an enormous contribution to improving the quality of labor and raising the rate of productivity; they can organize cooperatives, workers, banks and housing projects; they can help rural migrants make the adjustments to an industrial-urban environment; and they can serve as a training ground for leaders in community development and civic and political affairs generally.

The OAS is committed to helping unions play a constructive and positive role in national development.

In the Declaration of Cundinamarca of 1963, the First Inter-American Conference of Ministers of Labor stated: "There can be no effective economic and social planning unless the legitimate rights of labor are recognized and the aspirations of the workers are expressed in terms of concrete achievements involving wages, employment, working conditions, social security, health, housing, and education."

The amended OAS Charter commits the member states to the principle that "all human beings, without distinction . . .

have a right to material well-being and to their spiritual development under circumstances of liberty, dignity, equality of opportunity and economic security." The Charter also states that "work is a right and a social duty, it gives dignity to the one who performs it, and it should be performed under conditions, including a system of fair wages, that ensure life, health, and a decent standard of living for the worker and his family, both during his working years and in his old age, or when any circumstances deprive him of the possibility of working. . . ."

What has the OAS been doing to help member states achieve these objectives? It has been working with labor ministries, trade unions and vocational training institutions in an effort to strengthen the capacity of member states: (1) to plan more effectively in labor matters; (2) to stimulate popular participation in national planning efforts and in human resource boards and incomes and prices councils, and (3) to develop and administer programs which enable workers to share in the benefits of development.

To that end, the OAS Labor Program has sponsored a number of seminars and conferences, both national and international in scope, for trade-union and labor-ministry personnel.

At the same time, the OAS Labor Program is helping Latin American universities to strengthen teaching and research in labor economics and related fields, in order to increase the number of qualified graduates available to work in planning units, minimum wage systems, and mediation and inspection services of the ministries of labor, and in the research departments of the trade unions.

The Program has also helped workers' banks establish a foothold in Latin America with the objective of promoting workers' savings, satisfying their credit needs, protecting them against usury, and enabling them to participate directly in the development process.

The OAS commitment to social progress is being carried out in other areas as well. We have a cooperatives unit which is providing direct technical assistance to cooperatives and to government organizations concerned with their development. It has also set up demonstration projects in rural cooperatives in Brazil and Costa Rica and sponsored regional mobile courses and other types of courses on cooperatives in transportation, electrical production, housing, and other fields. It has arranged fellowships for administrators of cooperatives to study in other countries; and it has published a series of technical manuals to compensate for the lack of Spanish and Portuguese language textbooks of practical value to leaders and administrators of various types of cooperatives. The OAS has also devoted considerable effort to the training of personnel qualified to plan and execute community-development programs designed to stimulate maximum public participation. The staff has collaborated with schools of social work in revising their programs of study and field practices and it has arranged numerous fellowships, enabling specialists in this field to study in other countries of our own region as well as abroad.

*Auto mechanics
class in Haiti.
Latin America needs
to triple its
present number of skilled
workers by 1980.*

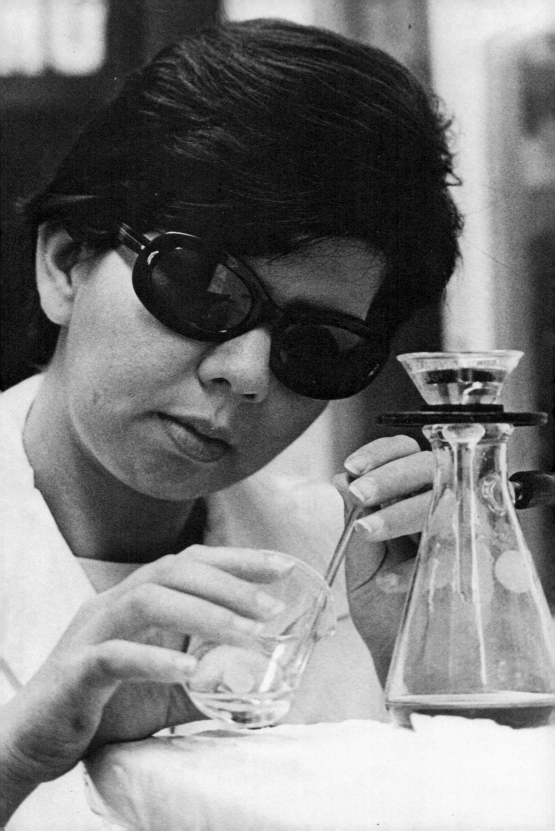

# CHAPTER 12

# THE PRODUCTIVITY GAP

One of the greatest obstacles to Latin American development today is low productivity on our farms and in our cities. We must achieve dramatic increases in our output. We must produce more and better products, and distribute them more widely at home and abroad. If we set our sights on higher productivity we will make simultaneous progress on a number of other problems, from malnutrition to inflation.

The task is by no means easy, and to accomplish it we must cope successfully with many related problems. Agricultural and industrial productivity can be increased to the desired levels only by massive efforts in technological transfer, education, and capital investment.

Professor W. Paul Strassmann of Michigan State University has defined technological change as the discovery and application of new or previously ignored or rejected production methods. He suggests that we view technology in terms of the Greek

A young Paraguayan scientist learns
new research techniques at the Puerto Rican Nuclear Center,
in a multinational project of the Regional Scientific
and Technological Development Program of the OAS.

concept of *techne,* with its connotation of man's combined intellectual, moral, and physiological ability to make a product. There is certain merit to this approach, because it induces us to view technology as the integrated function of man, method, and product.

Technological transfer in the developing countries today may involve breathtaking new discoveries or invention. More often, it consists of diffusion of routine advice about standard procedures. The most difficult part in the transfer process is adaptation of the methods and products to the requirements and resources peculiar to each country.

Even after adaptation to the local environment, the process of technological change frequently bogs down in the dissemination. Owing to the lack of efficient means for communication, many promising findings never get from the laboratory to the factory or the field where they can be put to use.

Technological progress in Latin America cannot go into high gear until we make some major quantitative and qualitative improvements in the area of education. Our programs in science, engineering, and vocational education are improving, but they have a long way to go to be on a par with our education in the humanities. Most universities are not sufficiently integrated into the economic life of their countries to contribute new knowledge for technological development.

A number of factors, including inadequate secondary-school preparation, limited facilities in the universities, and the plain economic facts of life keep most Latin American high school graduates from going to college. Only five percent of the university age population is enrolled in higher education. The favorite field of specialization continues to be law, which accounts for 25 percent of the university graduates. Unfortunately, the least popular fields are agronomy and architecture, which together account for only nine percent of graduates.

There is a serious shortage of skilled manpower at the subprofessional level—the technicians, foremen, research assistants, and extension agents. The low educational level of the working force makes it extremely difficult for competent supervisors to rise from the ranks and this is one of the reasons for the increased emphasis on vocational schools and on-the-job training.

In this connection, I should mention that United States industries are sending tools and equipment to some 150 Latin American vocational schools under the Tools for Freedom Program of the Pan American Development Foundation. This is an excellent example of private sector support, and it has prompted a number of Latin American industries to do likewise.

Despite the obstacles to technological progress in Latin America, there have been some large-scale successes. Here are a couple of examples.

Thanks to research at the Institute of Nutrition of Central America and Panama, low-cost basic foods, rich in vegetable protein, are now being manufactured in several Latin American countries under the generic name of Incaparina. Incaparina is almost as nutritious as milk and it has proved effective in preventing or curing protein malnutrition in children. The basic ingredients are grain—which can be wheat, rice, or any other cereal that is available locally—and oilseed meal, yeast, leaf meal (for vitamin A), and calcium carbonate. Another high-protein food now being widely distributed is CSM, which is made from corn, soya, and milk.

The breakthrough with dwarf wheat in Mexico has already been mentioned. There has also been a breakthrough with corn, a major diet item in many Latin American countries. Researchers discovered in the last decade that corn with two mutant genes which had been known for over thirty years is a rich source of two protein-building amino acids which are essential to animal and human nutrition. It actually has double the amount of these two amino acids to be found in normal corn. The new variety is called high-lysene corn. Tests show that when it is ground and prepared as bread or tortillas, it has the same protein value as skim milk, which can be of great importance in countries where corn is abundant and milk is scarce. Since presence of the mutant genes can be detected with the naked eye, cross breeding of high-lysene corn with local varieties is relatively simple. The new variety is already being grown and tested in Brazil, Colombia, and Guatemala.

Looking to the future, food technologists say that new foods are on the way: a meatlike soybean product, a palatable grass steak, hams and sausages from fishmeal, and protein supplements from petroleum. These will eventually compete in nutritive value, taste, and cost with the products of the farm. But while we are waiting for these new foods, there is a great deal that we must do to improve productivity as regards our existing foods. We could easily double agricultural productivity in Latin America by taking full advantage of the technological progress that has already been achieved in improved varieties of seeds and animal breeds, fertilizers, and pesticides, and elementary modern agricultural techniques. What the farmers need most of all is improved extension services and more reasonable sources of credit.

The Latin American governments are increasingly concerned with the need to reap maximum benefits from technology in both agriculture and industry. In some countries national research councils are cooperating actively with public, private, and university institutions. National science planning is in its infancy in Latin America, but at least it is under way.

Technological transfer frequently has multinational applications. Every country has something to teach and something to learn, and it is the task of the international organization to facilitate this process.

Although it is perhaps better known for its work to promote peace and security in the Americas, the Organization of American States is actually a major promoter of technological transfer in the hemisphere. Sixty-five percent of the Organization's resources are devoted to technical cooperation and regional development programs.

The OAS is a supplier of preinvestment services in the broadest sense of the term. These services include training, research, evaluation of natural resources, and assistance in actual development planning, which pave the way for feasibility studies and investment by international financing organizations and private capital.

Each member government presents to the OAS a National Technical Cooperation Program in accordance with its development needs. It is the governments, not the OAS, that decide what they need. The Program consists of a set of specific projects, ranked in order of priority, with projection of the needs for the following year. The General Secretariat of the

OAS studies the programs from the standpoint of the availability of funds, the structure of the services, and other feasibility criteria. Any adjustments required as a result of that evaluation are made by agreement between the member state and the General Secretariat.

The National Programs facilitate improved coordination within the OAS, within the countries themselves, and among international organizations. The OAS has recently taken steps for closer cooperation with the United Nations Development Program, the Inter-American Development Bank, FAO, UNESCO, and other organizations.

Two main types of technical cooperation are supplied by the OAS: advisory services and training. The advisory services consist of technical missions of three months to one year in duration, requested to deal with a specific development-related problem. Experts are recruited for the missions preferably, but not exclusively, from the member states. The program is sufficiently flexible to provide experts on short notice when problems of an emergency nature arise.

Simultaneously, the OAS is a major contributor to training for development. Its General Secretariat administers programs which currently train over 5,000 Latin American professionals each year. Before long that figure will be doubled by expanded activities in the area of education, science, and technology. The OAS already provides more than one-third of the total number of fellowships available to Latin America from public and private international sources.

A wide variety of training opportunities are available to meet the requirements of member states. First, there are the regional inter-American training centers, with headquarters in different Latin American countries. Each offers postgraduate training in a specific field, such as urban and regional planning, project development, statistics, land and water resource utilization, rural development and agrarian reform, public administration, or tax studies. In addition, there are special courses offered in nonmember states, for which the OAS provides travel grants, and the host country the other costs. These include, for example, educational administration in Great Britain, low-cost housing in Israel, and export promotion in Belgium. If a government desires personnel training in some specialization not covered by a regular course, the OAS grants individual fellowships for study or research at the postgraduate level in any member country of the OAS except the one of which the applicant is a citizen or permanent resident.

In addition to the above services provided directly by the national programs, the OAS is involved in cooperation with nonmember states in a series of technical cooperation integrated projects which have been identified by the OAS through the national planning offices of the member states and presented to possible donor governments by the OAS. Once accepted by the donors the OAS provides the cost of international travel and the donors the remaining costs.

Services to the member states were significantly expanded in 1969 with the launching of the Regional Educational Development Program and the Regional Scientific and Technological Development Program. These activities were established by the Inter-American Cultural Council (now Inter-American Council for Education, Science, and Culture) to enable the Latin American countries to speed up progress in these critical areas in accordance with the 1967 decision of the Meeting of American Chiefs of State.

The programs function mainly through multinational projects to strengthen and develop existing Latin American institutions. They provide visiting professors to reinforce existing staffs, and fellowships for the staffs to upgrade their knowledge and techniques so that they can replace the visiting professors when they leave. Modern equipment is provided where necessary. Each multinational center offers advanced training to other Latin American specialists in the field and promotes research, experimentation, and innovation. In addition to the support of the multinational centers, the programs provide grants to strengthen research institutions in selected fields.

Both programs are financed by the Special Multilateral Fund of the Inter-American Council for Education, Science, and Culture, whose general resources consist of voluntary contributions from member states, inter-American or international institutions, states not members of the Organization, universities, foundations, corporations, and individuals. The budgets for the two programs for 1970-71 total $15,000,000.

The Regional Educational Development Program is initially emphasizing four major fields: educational planning and administration; curricula improvement; vocational training; and modern educational technology, including educational television. The Regional Scientific and Technological Development Program is concentrating on postgraduate training in the basic sciences and engineering, and research on raw materials and applied technology.

We must not forget that the ultimate goal of technology is to offer man a richer, fuller life. In Latin America a hundred million people are still victims of poverty, ignorance, and disease. They deserve to enjoy the fruits of this amazing era of scientific progress, in which man has mastered the atom and the universe. The challenge calls for imaginative cooperation by all men of good will: international organizations, governments, universities, research centers, and industry. The task is great, but so too are the stakes: a world of want can never be a world at peace.

*Educational systems
throughout Latin America
are being modified
to prepare young people for
a more active role in
their country's development.
Rural normal school
at Rubio, Venezuela.*

# CHAPTER 13

# THE ECONOMIC DIMENSION OF EDUCATION

One of the most valuable resources in the economic process is man himself. Like hunger and disease, illiteracy and inadequate education are burdens that weigh heavily on the less-developed countries. Conversely, the educated man is a natural resource of the highest order. That is why education has not only a social function but an economic function.

Surprisingly, it is only recently that economists have come to see the vital importance of education in economic development and to speak of investment in human capital. Today they all recognize that the bottleneck in economic growth is the absence of an efficient, production-oriented educational system. Theodore Schultz, of the University of Chicago, has made studies that show that investment in education can bring about significant increases in production. He found that a dollar invested in educating a man often contributes more to national income than a dollar invested in communications, dams, machinery, or other capital goods.

Seen in this light, education takes on a new economic dimension and must be regarded as an investment of high priority.

In a free society in which the individual has the right to develop his potential capabilities in accordance with his own interests there may seem to be a contradiction between the concept of education for economic development and the concept of education as a social function. Actually there is no contradiction, because no one is forced to study in any particular specialization. If individual rights are respected and education is made available to all, in accordance with the interests of the individual, education can fulfill the social function while at the same time meeting the needs reflected in the economic development plans.

In countries with limited resources there is no justification for diverting scarce funds from other areas of investment to give priority to education unless education serves the cause of economic development in addition to carrying out its social mission. There is no reason to believe that a productive educational system cannot be a democratic system dedicated to human enrichment. There is no contradiction between the economic objectives of education and its human objectives.

Is education in Latin America doing its job? Is it preparing this generation and the next to manage an increasingly complex socioeconomic structure? Let us look at each of the educational levels individually.

The primary school, which is the foundation of the entire educational structure, must be efficient and must be open to all. The constitutions of the American Republics declare that elementary education is free and compulsory, and that all children, regardless of race, sex, creed, or social position, have a right to a primary education. But in practice this basic principle is not observed. As proof of this we have the alarming statistics concerning children of school age who are not in school.

There is a shortage of teachers and classrooms, and the methods and programs are not always designed to help a child develop his talents and learn the important characteristics of his home, his community, and his environment. Especially in the rural areas, where most Latin Americans live, schools retain traditional ideas and practices and children do not go beyond the third or fourth grade.

In many countries of the hemisphere there has been distinct progress in this area in recent years. All countries are aware of the seriousness of the problem and are struggling to solve it, but they still have a long way to go to meet the demands of economic and social development.

The weakest link in the educational system is the secondary level. In the last few decades there has been some progress in adapting secondary education to train a heterogeneous population in the ways of effective citizenship. However, there is still the heavy influence of an educational philosophy that dates from the colonial period, and which had as its goal the development of an intellectual elite capable of appreciating the arts, letters, and sciences. It stressed general culture and the classical subjects, but virtually ignored the applied sciences and vocational subjects. Its principal function was to prepare students for the university.

If we review the educational statistics we find that in Latin America less than five percent of the young people of university age are in universities. The rest, the vast majority, must stop in the middle of their education even though they are not equipped to earn a decent living. To serve this important segment of our youths, high schools must teach vocational skills and provide a terminal education as well as prepare students for the university.

Education for economic and social development must go beyond the traditional university disciplines to training for all trades and professions, from carpenters, electricians, and specialized workers to doctors, engineers, and research workers, including shop foremen, accountants, and secretaries, and a host of other occupations at all levels. All have a role in development.

Vocational education is indispensable for growth in trade and industry, and, until it becomes an integral part of secondary education and is no longer treated as a poor relative, we will waste the resources of a sizeable group of the population that does not complete its education. Consequently, one of the highest priorities in educational planning should be assigned to vocational education at the middle level.

The development process requires the training of the present generation as well as future generations. Specifically, the current labor force, which in some cases is barely participating in the economic process.

Although there are a number of opportunities for professional people to keep up to date in their fields through technical publications, a short course or a lecture series, more must be done to tap the bulk of human capital that is underused and practically wasted: the unskilled workers who for want of an opportunity have not been able to develop their potential in a given craft or trade.

Some countries, particularly Argentina, Brazil, Colombia, Peru, and Venezuela, have organized outstanding industrial training programs to deal with this problem. The specialized training is opening up new opportunities for the workers and enabling them to make a more positive contribution to their nation's economy.

Let us consider now the universities.

By the beginning of the thirteenth century two main types of universities had emerged in Europe. The University of Paris was a corporation of professors, which enforced the regulations that they had established and defended the university's rights against the Crown and the Pope. By contrast, the University of Bologna was actually a student guild that had assumed the function of organizing the university and hiring the professors. Institutions of the latter type died out in Europe and now all of the universities in Europe and the United States are descendants of the University of Paris. In Latin America, however, most of the universities have tended to follow the early lines of the University of Bologna.

The problems posed by a politically active student body are not confined to Latin America, as recent events in the United States have shown, but Latin American students have a much older tradition of political action. They fought first against the Crown and the Church, which dominated the university completely during the colonial period, and later against all kinds of dictatorships. When the university achieved its political and intellectual autonomy, the students became its jealous guardians. The students are proud of their libertarian spirit, their rejection of dictatorships, and their constant concern with social reform. They have tried to protect the university from the political instability that has so frequently surrounded it, but often they have achieved the opposite result and brought politics into the classroom. The intensive political atmosphere is not conducive to study or to a high quality of education. Furthermore, the excessive participation of the student body in the government of the university sometimes results in situations reminiscent of the medieval University of Bologna.

Since public universities are generally tuition-free, they are open to people of all income levels, although in some countries students must take competitive entrance examinations because the number of vacant places is limited. One might think that the healthy influence of students from all walks of life would cause the university to be more oriented toward the nation's needs, but in reality the students usually become a part of the aloof establishment.

Another problem is the existence of large numbers of part-time professors and part-time students. A university professorship is an honor that is poorly remunerated, so a professor has to supplement his income with other jobs. This fact explains the absence of a nucleus that lives, thinks, and dreams in the university on a permanent basis, which the university must have if it is to be a dynamic and creative force in a changing society. In the majority of cases, the university is a way station for both professors and students whose real interests lie elsewhere.

University budgets are generally inadequate to meet growing demands, and traditional defects in organization often lead to further dilution of these resources through dispersion and duplication.

On the positive side, there are some outstanding examples in Latin America of how a university, struggling with all kinds of obstacles and overcoming the forces of tradition, has placed itself at the service of the community. In the majority of cases, though, the students are still not receiving an education that will equip them to assume responsibilities in the new socio-economic patterns that must emerge if we are to solve the basic problems of the region.

In some countries, such as Chile, students have carried out far-reaching volunteer social service projects in both urban slums and rural areas.

The principal objective of the university in the process of economic development is to serve the community. Its curricula must be broadened to meet the multiple demands of modern society. Basic and applied research must be an integral part of the university's work. Extension programs must be improved so that useful concepts can be transmitted to the entire population.

Because of their limited means and the shortage of specialized professors, most Latin American universities do not offer training in many technological fields or conduct research designed to speed up the development process. The universities need more technically qualified faculty members, more and better research facilities and laboratories, and better organization.

In the foreseeable future we will not have the vast financial resources that would be required to equip all Latin American universities adequately. To provide facilities for 8.6 percent of the university-age students by 1975, it has been estimated that between 1966 and 1975 the Latin American universities would need to spend $7.5 billion for current expenses and $1.5 billion for capital improvements.

The magnitude of Latin America's educational problems and the lack of national resources to cope with them has led the governments in recent years to place increasing emphasis on the multilateral approach and the pooling of resources in regional centers.

The OAS Regional Educational Development Program and the Regional Scientific and Technological Development Program, which are now in full swing, were described in the preceding chapter.

The regional centers of these programs have an international faculty and international student body. By pooling economic resources and eliminating costly duplication of effort, and by bringing together the finest professors of the hemisphere and elsewhere, the regional centers can offer the same opportunities as the most distinguished universities of the world.

Think what it means to the students to be able to pursue advanced studies in their own language and environment. Formerly, students in the technical disciplines often had to go to the United States or Europe for graduate study, where they faced a language barrier and they conducted research in a strange environment—research that was often hard to apply in their own countries. The late Max Millikan of MIT pointed out that although the basic laws of physics are universal, the adaptation of those laws to the design of a piece for a specific use in a given environment, with its own resources and its peculiar psychological and cultural framework, is as difficult as the discovery of the basic laws. He also said that there are problems in the philosophy of education that are universal, but the planning of educational methods effectively geared to the given environment requires a specific act of inventive adaptation.

The students who are most successful in adapting to the foreign environment during their graduate study often fail to return to their native country, which needs them badly and has invested a great deal in their basic education. These graduates find jobs abroad that offer irresistible opportunities and better pay than they could expect at home. The exodus of Latin American scientists and professional people to the United States and Europe, commonly called the "brain drain," will be drastically reduced as more students have the opportunity to complete their studies in their own region.

Universities in Latin America will also benefit from the regional centers, because they will be able to concentrate their limited resources on improving the quality of education in the disciplines for which they will continue to be responsible. This concentration of resources may significantly improve the quality of basic education.

*Democracy works if given a chance,*
*because people are*
*fundamentally democratic. Colombian Indians*
*exercise right to vote.*

# CHAPTER 14

# OUR COMMITMENT TO DEMOCRACY

"**F**ree men working through the institution of representative democracy can best satisfy man's aspirations, including those for work, home and land, health and schools." This is the basic principle underlying the Alliance for Progress, as stated in the Declaration to the Peoples of America that accompanied the Charter of Punta del Este in 1961. The Declaration enumerated a long list of goals, and at the top of the list was: "to improve and strengthen democratic institutions through application of the principle of self-determination by the people."

Historically the establishment of democratic forms of government has been difficult in Latin America. At the time we won our independence our inexperience in the practice of democratic government was as great as our love of freedom. In contrast to the relative freedom and self-government enjoyed by the colonies of North America, we were the victims of despotism firmly entrenched by such institutions as a feudal system of land tenure, a politically strong military class which emerged out of the wars for independence, a highly centralized and paternalistic government, and a powerful church that dominated education and intervened in politics. In some areas the origin of the authoritarian tradition can be traced back before the Colonial period to the original inhabitants of the region.

These historical obstacles help to explain why it sometimes seems that democracy in Latin America is taking one or two steps backward for every step forward, and why there have been too many changes of government in some countries and not enough in others.

What is democratic government? The concept of government by the people, through their freely elected representatives, is manifest in many forms and degrees. There is no single model that is universally valid or desirable. Even countries that seem to have advanced well along the road of democracy are forced to admit that their democratic institutions are capable of further perfection, and that what has worked well for them may not work well elsewhere.

There are nonetheless some general guidelines for the identification of democratic governments within the inter-American system. They were stated for the benefit of "national and international public opinion" in the Declaration of Santiago, approved at the Fifth Meeting of Consultation of Ministers of Foreign Affairs in 1959.

Among others, the following essential characteristics of a democratic government are singled out in the Declaration: separation of powers, rule of law, free elections, fixed terms of office and nonperpetuation in power, respect for human rights, social justice, and freedom of information and expression.

There are a number of Latin American countries that have met these criteria for years, but unfortunately there are some where democracy is precarious or nonexistent. Some of the most ardent speeches about democratic principles are made by representatives of the least democratic governments.

Why is the *coup d'état* still with us?

One reason that we hear is that some countries are not "ready" for democracy because they have high rates of illiteracy, a small middle class, and large unassimilated rural populations. Superficially this reason seems plausible, but there are doubts about the extent of its validity when we apply it to the reality in Latin America. On the one hand we find a chronic absence of democratic government in some countries with high literacy rates, large middle classes, and small rural populations; on the other, we find democratic governments in some countries that lack one or more of these conditions. Those who place excessive faith in education as a prerequisite for democracy should not overlook the fact that unfortunately there are many highly educated citizens who find it convenient to tolerate, and even collaborate with, a dictator. Clearly education is only part of the problem.

It has been said that in countries where only the literate, advantaged classes can vote a conscientious military regime might be more representative than a bad government elected behind a facade of democratic institutions. This is true, but the solution lies not in accepting the military regime as inevitable but in broadening the electoral base and making democracy a reality rather than a facade.

It is also frequently claimed that dictatorships continue to thrive because the United States aids and abets them, in the name of stability. However, if the United States withdraws aid from a *de facto* government to demonstrate displeasure, it is accused of intervening in that state's internal affairs and trying to dictate its form of government. External aid may be of great help to a dictatorship, but it may not be the deciding factor in the regime's perpetuation. There have been cases where dictatorial regimes have survived for years without significant U.S. aid, and other cases where dictatorial regimes aided by the United States have been rather short-lived.

Democratic aspirations and principles notwithstanding, some Latin American countries have a long-standing tradition of changing governments by force. The reasons for the tradition are many. The military forces are often the most powerful group within a country, and they may have a broad interpretation of their mandate to maintain order. Some people have grown accustomed to an authoritarian yet paternalistic government that protects them—if they don't dissent—and cares for them without requiring much participation on their part. The personalistic pattern in politics has encouraged demagogues and made it difficult to maintain political parties based on issues rather than individuals. When elections are held, voters frequently view them with suspicion because they fear that the ballot may be manipulated to serve certain interests, and that, even if the voting is honest, the generals, admirals, and marshals may not accept the results.

It has been said: "Whenever the people grow weary of the existing government, they can exercise their constitutional right of amending it, or their revolutionary right to dismember or overthrow it." That radical statement was made not by a Latin American but by Abraham Lincoln, in his first inaugural address.

The question is, how can we distinguish between a popular government and an unpopular one? How can a military government prove that it is "of the people, by the people, and for the people" unless it submits to the acid test of the ballot box?

A U.S. author and diplomat, John B. Martin, has suggested, perhaps jestingly, a constitutional alternative to the *coup d' état*. It is a novel procedure to permit rapid changes of government in the event of popular dissatisfaction with a regime. At the end of his first year in office the president would have to face an automatic referendum on the question, "do you approve the way the president is doing his job?" If the answer is "no" he must schedule a new election within thirty days and could not be a candidate himself. If the answer is "yes" he would continue two more years and then face another referendum. His term would end after five years. This procedure might reduce the incidence of unconstitutional coups, and provide for a more genuine democracy, but of course it is doubtful that a nation's best interests would be served by institutionalizing political instability.

It is true that many factors conspire against the consolidation of democratic regimes, but this is no cause for pessimism. Where there is a will, the obstacles can be overcome. Democratic government can blossom out if given a chance, because people are fundamentally democratic. The author knows from his term as President of Ecuador that to govern democratically is to do it the hard way; it takes longer to accomplish things, but progress is steadier and of a more solid nature.

It is not possible to flick a few switches and turn on democratic institutions. They do not spring forth full-grown like Minerva, but must be painstakingly cultivated. The magnitude of the task is no justification for failure to attempt it. Even in countries where national political freedom is somewhat restricted, it may be possible for democratic institutions to get a toehold on the local level, through civic organizations, trade unions, and parent-teacher associations. This type of citizen participation to achieve desired ends can go a long way to develop a democratic tradition of responsibility that can later serve as a firm foundation for strengthening democratic institutions on the national level.

The late Max F. Millikan pointed out that a sound democracy depends heavily on the strength and number of institutions that stand between the individual and the national government, defending his individual rights in the process of defending institutional interests.

The doctrine of the Alliance for Progress states that democracy is the best way to achieve socioeconomic progress. Of course it is not the only way, because dictators of the right or left can also bring about increases in per capita income, improved housing and education standards, and a redistribution of wealth. But progress in a climate of oppression is sterile, and progress is easier if the people are active and willing participants.

Ideally, democracy and socioeconomic development in Latin America should be simultaneous and mutually reinforcing. Democracy will not be meaningful until a certain level of economic growth is attained. Democracy is a hollow word to an illiterate peasant who doesn't know where his next meal is coming from.

Democracy is on trial in Latin America. If it fails to satisfy the longing of millions for a better standard of living, accumulated frustration will cause people to reject it. In essence, in our time democracy without a social conscience is not democracy. Citizens and leaders who are concerned exclusively with protection of their own rights cannot make democracy work; they must make it possible for all the people to attain a decent level of well-being in a climate of freedom.

Is there a collective responsibility within the inter-American system for promoting representative democracy in the Americas, or for discouraging *de facto* governments? Since the effective exercise of representative democracy is one of the principles enshrined in the Charter of the OAS, and it has been demonstrated more than once that non-democratic governments can constitute a threat to the peace and security of the hemisphere, it is generally conceded that there is a common interest in the prevalence of democracy. There are widely differing opinions, however, on the measures that should be taken to promote that interest.

Those who oppose collective action in defense of democracy consider that the OAS Charter principles are declarations of aims rather than contractual obligations, and that nonrecognition would constitute an attempt to intervene in a sovereign state's internal affairs, which is expressly proscribed by the Charter. A Latin American foreign minister made this point plainly when he said that his government ''prefers to have occasional interruptions of the democratic system rather than violate the principles of nonintervention and self-determination.''

On the other hand, there have been proposals in the OAS dating back to 1945 to use nonrecognition of *de facto* governments as a way to promote democracy and respect for human rights. Fourteen years later the Fifth Meeting of Consultation of

Ministers of Foreign Affairs requested the OAS Council to prepare a draft convention on the effective exercise of representative democracy. A seven-nation committee wrote a draft, but
when it was circulated among the governments for their opinions it received little support.

The Second Special Inter-American Conference (1965) approved a resolution recommending an informal procedure on
the recognition of de facto governments. In the event of the
overthrow of a government, the member states are immediately
to begin an exchange of views on the situation, taking into
consideration whether foreign intervention was involved and
whether the new government proposes to hold elections "within
a reasonable period" and agrees to fulfill its country's international obligations, respect human rights, and comply with
the commitments of the Alliance for Progress. After opinions
have been exchanged each government decides whether it
will maintain diplomatic relations with the new government.

This resolution, introduced by Costa Rica, was approved by
a vote of 14 in favor, none against, and five abstentions. It
goes too far for the most ardent defenders of nonintervention,
but at the same time it falls short of the mark for the governments that would like to institutionalize a process of collective
nonrecognition of undemocratic governments.

The author shares the view of former OAS Secretary General Alberto Lleras Camargo: "Where one must combat coups
is inside each country—by lessening demagoguery, upholding
the authority of the laws, and eradicating the pretexts under
which coups are produced. . . . There must be a great American
conscience against coups d'état before the OAS can be put

into action. To begin by taking international action in order to create this conscience could be a fatal error."

Nonrecognition of governments, even if it were to attain wider acceptance as a mechanism, is a negative approach to the problem. There have been some suggestions for a positive approach, such as the recommendation of the Special Consultative Committee on Security for an "ideological offensive" to convince the peoples of the Americas "that the only final answer to the permanent threat of communism lies in the development of a true democratic conscience, the establishment of basic educational levels, and the solution of urgent economic problems by stable democratic governments."

Thus far we have not undertaken an "ideological offensive" *per se,* but we are using various positive means within the inter-American community to promote democracy. We are stimulating economic development in order to improve the well-being of the people of Latin America and to equip them to participate more effectively in the democratic process. As part of this effort, a private foundation associated with the OAS, the Pan American Development Foundation, specializes in loans for grass-roots development projects in Latin America that are serving to bring millions of people together in the democratic institutions of the community-building process. The Inter-American Commission on Human Rights has been working actively to promote respect for basic human rights and will have increased responsibility under an inter-American convention on human rights that was signed in San José, Costa Rica in 1969 and is pending ratification by the member states. Another contribution to the strengthening of democracy is the missions that have been sent by the OAS General Secretariat upon requests from several countries to provide technical assistance to governments in the establishment of election procedures or to observe the actual registration and voting.

Although the international community can help in a variety of ways, the basic responsibility for the development of democratic institutions lies with the people and government of each country. Democracy cannot be imposed, but it can be nurtured. There will be setbacks and imperfections, and many variations to suit local conditions, but our commitment to democracy will be strengthened in the years ahead.

*First Special Session
of the General Assembly
under the amended
Charter of the Organization
of American States, July 1970.
Hall of the Americas,
Pan American Union Building,
Washington, D. C.*

The Pan American
Union Building, or
"House of the Americas,"
in Washington, D.C.,
is the headquarters
of the Organization
of American States.

# CHAPTER 15

# THE NEW ORGANIZATION OF AMERICAN STATES

The principal vehicle for multilateral cooperation in the Americas is the Organization of American States, which had its origin in 1890 and is the oldest of the world's regional international organizations.

The twin objectives of the OAS, according to its Charter, are to preserve the peace and security of the member states and to promote, by cooperative action, their economic, social, and cultural development.

Today, without neglecting its important responsibilities in the areas of peace and security, the OAS is increasing its emphasis on the problems of economic and social development. It was decided in 1965 that the time had come "to forge a new dynamism for the inter-American system." This led to the drafting of a number of amendments to the OAS Charter, which were approved in February, 1967 at a Special Inter-American Conference in Buenos Aires, Argentina. The amendments are contained in the Protocol of Buenos Aires, which entered into force on February 27, 1970, upon deposit of the required number of ratifications.

The amendments to the OAS Charter fall into two general categories. The first includes changes in the chapters dealing with "standards," which are basically declarations of objectives by the member states. The second type is the institutional change, which affects the structure of the OAS.

Let us look first at the standards.

The economic and social standards in the Protocol of Buenos Aires are more numerous and more specific than those contained in the Charter of 1948. The basic principle is that the member states pledge to make a united effort to ensure social justice in the hemisphere and dynamic and balanced economic development for their peoples, as conditions essential to peace and security.

Other economic standards are these: When aid is granted, it should be provided under flexible conditions, with special attention to the relatively less developed countries. The member states should avoid policies that hurt the economic development of another member state, and they should join together to help a member state affected by economic difficulties that cannot be remedied through its own efforts.

In the area of trade, the amendments call for reduction or elimination of restrictions on exports, agreements to ensure improved conditions for trade in basic commodities, a means to lessen the adverse effects of sharp fluctuations in export earnings, and expansion of export opportunities for manufactured and semimanufactured products. When the more developed countries grant tariff concessions in international trade agreements that benefit the less-developed countries, they should not expect reciprocal concessions from those countries that are incompatible with their economic development, financial, and trade needs.

The Protocol of Buenos Aires, reflecting the call to a new dimension of patriotism, declares that Latin American integration is an objective of the inter-American system. It declares that the member states will take the necessary measures to establish a Latin American common market in the shortest possible time. The member states agree to accelerate integration in all its aspects, to give adequate priority to multinational projects, and to encourage economic and financial institutions of the inter-American system to support regional integration institutions and programs. The principal inter-American financial institution is the Inter-American Development Bank, which was established in 1959 with the assistance of the OAS, and properly calls itself "the bank of integration."

The chapter on social standards in the amended Charter retains the declaration of the Charter of 1948 that all human beings have a right to material well-being and to their spiritual development under circumstances of liberty, dignity, equality of opportunity, and economic security. The amendments go on to stress the need for action in several fields, such as labor relations, social security, and the full integration of the national community, including isolated sectors of the population.

In keeping with the concept of integral development, the Protocol of Buenos Aires replaced the Bogotá Charter's brief reference to cultural standards with a chapter on educational, scientific, and cultural standards. In addition to objectives in elementary, secondary, and university education, the chapter refers to the need for special attention to the eradication of illiteracy, strengthening of adult and vocational education, and the role of scientific institutions and cultural exchange.

Perhaps the major structural change in the amended Charter is the creation of the General Assembly, which replaces the Inter-American Conference as the highest organ of the OAS. The Inter-American Conference was supposed to meet once every five years, but in practice that was not the case. The last regular Inter-American Conference was held in 1954. The new General Assembly will meet at least once a year, to provide effective high-level coordination of the inter-American system. Normally the annual session of the General Assembly will be held in a different member state each year. If for any reason the Assembly cannot meet in the country chosen, or in an alternate, it will meet at the headquarters of the General Secretariat.

In addition to providing overall policy direction for the OAS, the General Assembly has the following functions, formerly carried out by the OAS Council: approve the program-budget of the Organization; coordinate the activities of its organs, agencies, and entities; promote cooperation with the United Nations and other international organizations; adopt general standards to govern the operations of the General Secretariat; elect the Secretary General and Assistant Secretary General; and approve the admission of new member states.

Another striking change in the organization chart of the OAS concerns two Councils that were formerly subsidiary organs of the OAS Council: the Inter-American Economic and Social Council, and the Inter-American Cultural Council, whose name was changed to the Inter-American Council for Education, Science, and Culture. Reflecting the high priority assigned to their function, these organs are now directly responsible to the General Assembly.

Each of these two Councils has a permanent committee composed of a Chairman and a minimum of seven other members. Each member is nominated by a country or group of countries. The Inter-American Committee on the Alliance for Progress, known by its Spanish initials as CIAP, serves as the permanent committee of the Economic and Social Council.

CIAP has earned a high reputation in the international development-financing community for its annual country reviews, which examine each nation's economic and social progress and analyze requirements for external aid in support of national efforts. Since 1966 the United States Congress has required that all appropriations for U.S. aid to Latin America take into account the findings of CIAP.

The Economic and Social Council is responsible for adopting OAS programs in the economic and social areas including those of the Special Development Assistance Fund, which channels voluntary contributions from the member governments into multinational programs of technical assistance in areas of key importance to the member states' development.

The Inter-American Council for Education, Science, and Culture is responsible for OAS activities in its area of competence, including the regional programs in education, science, and technology. (See Chapter 12.)

Other changes in the Protocol of Buenos Aires affect the Permanent Council, as the former Council of the Organization is now called. Although some of its functions were passed to the General Assembly, the Council has new responsibilities in the area of peaceful settlement of disputes. It will use the services of an Inter-American Committee on Peaceful Settlement, which supersedes the Inter-American Peace Committee and has new authority to offer its good offices at the request of a single party to a dispute. The Permanent Council also plays an important role as Preparatory Committee of the General Assembly.

The public often confuses the roles of the General Secretariat and the deliberative bodies of the OAS. The latter are composed of representatives of the governments, engaged in multilateral diplomacy in which no country has a veto and matters are resolved by agreement. The General Secretariat, which backstops the other organs of the OAS and helps to execute their decisions, is not a political body but a technical and administrative one. Its international civil servants—about 1,300 in all—are responsible to the Secretary General and not to their respective governments.

What is the role of the General Secretariat of the OAS under the Protocol? The Secretariat will continue to be the central and permanent organ of the OAS, but it will have vastly increased responsibilities to provide research and support services in a coordinated manner for all of the other organs, and it will be responsible to the General Assembly.

Under the Protocol of Buenos Aires the General Secretariat is no longer known as the Pan American Union. Although the name Pan American Union had a long-standing tradition in the inter-American system, since 1948 the public had always been confused about the relationship of the Pan American Union to the OAS. Hopefully, elimination of the name will help to eliminate the confusion.

But the name is not the only thing that changed in the General Secretariat. To support improved and expanded services to the member states, it was necessary for the OAS General Secretariat to effect a significant upgrading of its internal capability and to institute modern management techniques. Accordingly, the General Secretariat has been reorganized, consolidating and rationalizing its programs and introducing systems for effective programming and performance monitoring. The new systems enable the member states to see exactly how their money is being used and to evaluate its impact, and to project the requirements for at least six years ahead. The budget proposal for the 1970-72 biennium recommends that the number of the General Secretariat's programs be reduced from 31 to 16. This concentration of efforts will permit maximum impact and highest quality services from the resources available, and avoid duplication of activities that are being carried out by other organizations.

The member states have indicated that they are pleased with the changes that are taking place in the OAS, and their leaders have pledged their full support of the regional organization in its continuing process of adaptation to meet the changing needs of the times.

We know the OAS is far from perfect. It mirrors the imperfections, hopes, fears, and frustrations of the governments that comprise it. But it is the best tool we have for multilateral cooperation in the Americas, and wherever it can be improved, we will improve it.

*The earth as seen from a weather satellite 22,300 miles above Brazil.*
*Northern coastline of South America is clearly visible in center of globe.*

# CHAPTER 16

# ONE WORLD

When the Apollo astronauts circling the moon looked back to earth, seeing a small, distant planet with its particular geography, they gained a unique perspective: one world, in which basic ties of fraternity and solidarity unite all the people traveling together on a single lonely planet in the enormity of space. This is a fitting perspective, as we venture into the closing third of the twentieth century, building on the remarkable achievements of the first two-thirds. In this period we must produce more and distribute that production more equitably—moving ahead with all our ingenuity and dedication to achieve a better life for all people and peace for all nations.

Unfortunately, the image of unity is abruptly shattered when we view the earth from its surface rather than from the perspective of space. We see a planet which, despite great technological advances, is marked by the differences among men: not only geographic differences, but differences that man has made but not bridged.

A number of man-made gaps fracture our shrinking planet and constitute formidable barriers to peace and progress: the poverty gap, the ideological gap, and the technology gap. They are perpetuated and unfortunately even widened by several other gaps of our times:

- An unsatisfactory system of trade and trade policies
- Polarization and concentration of capital
- Inflation
- The shortage of qualified administrators
- The education gap, at all levels
- The health gap
- Population growth rates that are too high in some areas and too low in others

As we move to surmount these gaps, to reach better understanding, we must acknowledge that the world is not headed toward the imposition of a single point of view which will be the common denominator for all people. Our world is moving toward regionalism—but this regionalism will be the basis for more meaningful worldwide cooperation. If each region will take a hard, close look at itself—and act on the basis of its findings—the coming decade will be decisive in setting the tone for growth and cooperation on our planet.

In Latin America we share with other peoples of the world the effects of the political, technological, and social revolution of our era. We are known for our rapid population growth, which gives a youthful profile to our peoples. Like so many other countries, we are facing the revolution of rising expectations that has shaken the underdeveloped world.

Contrary to the experience of certain African and Asian groups, however, we have been politically independent for about a century and a half. Our nationalism has deep roots. Our collective action is based on the ideals of union that were expressed at the dawn of our independence. To a certain extent, our work is to bring up to date our rich heritage and endow it with a modern spirit, so that we may enjoy the benefits of technological progress.

In the face of enormous social pressures and urgent demands, our mission is not to create a state for the first time but rather to restructure the entire framework of secular institutions that our leaders of independence gave us, so that the *raison d'etre* of each state may respond to present-day requirements.

We are engaged in an enormous effort at modernization in which we must reconcile the tradition that supports the foundation of our nationalities with the requirements of social and economic change and the changes brought about by the technological revolution that is being felt, to a greater or lesser extent, in all our countries.

The need for change appears first of all in the national scene. The national effort must be the starting point of this entire struggle to establish a new structure in the Latin American world. But we must also remember that throughout independent life we have developed a unique system of international relations. We have established certain legal and juridical principles and traditions which also form part of our hemispheric heritage. Here, too, we are not at the stage of initiation and of trial and error. We have a heritage that is reflected in important conquests, a heritage that requires a new surge of effort, a process of adaptation to the requirements of present-day international cooperation.

In the past decade enormous changes have occurred in the political and ideological spectrum of the world. Ten years ago, few would have foreseen the breakthroughs in science, the changes of the international financial system now taking place, the persistence of the United States balance-of-payments problem, the setbacks in moving toward free and nondiscriminatory trade, the drama of the population explosion, or the emergence of the problems of youth and urbanization, which are common to developed and developing countries alike.

Pervasive as these events are, they influence but do not alter the basis of the special relationship of solidarity that exists, and must continue to exist, among all the countries of the hemisphere, for mutual benefit. That relationship is based on the undeniable facts of history, geography, and shared aspirations which are the foundations of our inter-American system. That system has evolved over many decades and has withstood many strains. But it is clear that to become stronger it must evolve further, adapting to the new events and circumstances. And as the world becomes ever more interdependent, Latin America also is drawn more and more to the center of the stage; therefore, our regional system must broaden its horizons and become ever more outward-looking. In this sense the recent admission of Trinidad and Tobago, Barbados and Jamaica to membership in the OAS, together with the hope that Canada will also join soon, takes on special importance. Equally significant for our system is the need to strengthen further our ties with Europe and other parts of the world, as well as with the United Nations, so as to speed the development of Latin America as an integral part of the western community of nations.

Even in countries with a relatively low birth rate,
such as Argentina, migration from the provinces
is swelling the population of the capitals.
Calle Florida, Buenos Aires.

*The basic objective*
*of the Latin American countries*
*in the seventies is*
*to raise the standard of living*
*of their people faster*
*than ever before.*
*Safe water supply comes to a*
*village in Guanajuato, Mexico.*

# CHAPTER 17

# COOPERATION...
# NOT CHARITY

With all the progress in Latin America to date, per capita annual income for the region as a whole is still only about $400; one in three Latin American adults is illiterate; and a Latin American baby is three times as likely to die before his fifth birthday as a baby born in the United States or Canada. The basic policy objective of the Latin American countries in the seventies is simply this: to continue to raise the standard of living of their people and to do it faster than ever before.

The emphasis in Latin America today is on integral development, concerned not only with economic and social factors, but with a balanced improvement in the quality of the society, with due consideration for education, technology, and the strengthening of positive cultural values.

A number of Latin America's specific goals in the seventies were mentioned in the preceding chapters; to increase productivity in the factories and on the farms; to educate people for development; to reduce the ranks of the unemployed; to increase and diversify exports; to establish multi-national enterprises; to upgrade scientific and technological research; to accelerate regional integration; to strengthen democratic institutions; and to obtain more genuine cooperation for development from the world's industrialized nations.

Latin America's population growth rate continues to be the highest in the world, estimated at 2.8 percent per year. At this rate the region's population will almost triple by the end of the century. In the years immediately ahead, the population will increase by roughly 8,000,000 per annum. If death rates continue to fall faster than birth rates, as the experts predict, even the rate of population growth will increase. This problem is aggravated by the youthful profile of the population. It is predicted that throughout the seventies 42 percent of Latin America's population will be under 15 years of age. The Latin American countries could produce enough food to cope with the projected increase of the population, thanks to the "green revolution," but they could probably not provide adequate housing, education, and health services to the expanded population. They would be hard put to make up existing deficits in these areas with zero population growth. These are problems that must be taken into account by development planners in the seventies.

The search for mutually satisfactory relationships among the nations of this hemisphere has been a long and rocky one, frustrated at times by intervention, resentment, and conflict. Over the years, however, the inter-American system has matured to the point where the countries can effectively negotiate their differences. This is truly a remarkable accomplishment.

Relations between the United States and Latin America in the seventies will have to take into account the emerging unity of purpose among the Latin American nations. Today Latin America is more united and more cohesive than ever before. The countries recognize an identity of interest and the need to negotiate and cooperate with the United States on the basis of equality, dignity, and reciprocity.

The Latin American countries seek cooperation not charity; dignity not dependence; and interest not intervention. These desires are just and reasonable, and they should guide our actions in the Americas in the coming decade.

There are bound to be actions by the Latin American countries, in the pursuit of their legitimate interests, which, in the short run, may adversely affect certain interests in the United States. However, there is hope for reason and moderation on both sides. Retaliation by the United States will not eliminate the actions; it will fan the flames of nationalism and aggravate the situation. In a word, the key to improved relations is understanding—understanding about what constitutes, in the long run, the best interests of both the United States and Latin America.

There is one point on which leaders in both Latin America and the United States agree: it is necessary to work toward self-sustaining economic growth in Latin America, so that the region may no longer be dependent upon external financial assistance. But if the leaders agree on the objective, they do not see eye to eye on the means for its achievement. Some would place the emphasis on aid, others on trade, and still others on private investment.

President Nixon has announced a new approach on the part of the United States which could contribute to a major reordering of inter-American relations in the seventies. The approach is based on the concept that the Latin American countries can and should plan their own development and shape their own destiny. This nonpaternalistic attitude is a promising sign.

There are three other signs which augur well for improved relations in the seventies. One is the decision by the U. S. Government to permit CIAP to review its development assistance to Latin America. The second sign is the fact that governments in both the United States and Latin America are putting generalities aside and dealing with specific issues, thorny though they may be, instead of trying to sweep them under the rug. The final promising sign is the new process of multinational negotiation of these issues by the Special Committee for Consultation and Negotiation of the Inter-American Economic and Social Council.

We need to discuss the issues frankly and realistically, that is, to negotiate. We need to develop positive attitudes and discard stereotypes. At the same time, we need to mobilize our resources—human, technical, and financial—more efficiently and more effectively than we ever have before.

The peoples of the Americas, their governments, and the OAS must all work together with a new dimension of patriotism, to attack the evils of underdevelopment with renewed vigor and faith. We all have a role to play in the common effort. It is a time for hope, a time for faith, and a time for sacrifice.

In the early days of the Alliance for Progress it was said that it is "one minute to midnight" in Latin America. The word midnight suggested the imminence of violent revolution and communist takeover. Although that possibility may continue to plague us, we must not be alarmists, but realists. It is not one minute to midnight today. Instead, we are in the forenoon of a struggle that may last for many years. The goal is clear: social and economic development within a framework of freedom and justice. What is not clear is how long it will take to reach that goal, and whether at some point frustration may invite alternative and less desirable solutions.

As we push forward together, we must not harbor the illusion that prosperity for all of Latin America is just around the corner. The most optimistic projections, envisioning a reduction of the rate of population growth to two percent, foresee an average per capita income of $1,500 by the year 2000. This would be a significant improvement over the present figure of about $400, but still well below the present per-capita income in the industrialized countries, which is $2,500.

The point is, even with sustained domestic effort and generous external cooperation the improvement of the standard of living of the man in the street will not be spectacular on a year-to-year basis. Over the course of a generation, however, progress can be significant. Our children will reap the benefits of the effort.

We must not dwell on the failures of the past, but on the opportunities that lie ahead. If the statesmen, parliaments, and peoples of the Americas will but respond with vision to the challenges of our time, in a spirit of mutual trust and honest cooperation, the New World will fulfill its historic destiny.

*Satellite tracking station
in Mexico symbolizes
effort to expand
telecommunications
in Latin America.*

# APPENDIX

# PROFILES OF THE LATIN AMERICAN NATIONS

The sketches on the pages that follow present a panoramic overview of the geography, history, culture, and economy of the Latin American member states of the Organization of American States. Highly selective and limited to the highlights, the capsule descriptions nevertheless demonstrate the unity and diversity that is Latin America.

The profiles were prepared with the cooperation of the Department of Cultural Affairs and the Department of Information and Public Affairs of the Organization of American States.

**ARGENTINA**
Population: 24.3 million

VAST AND RICH in natural resources, Argentina is a progressive and socially homogeneous nation of great cultural activity. Its capital, Buenos Aires, is the largest Spanish-speaking city in the world.

**Geography.** The temperate region of the northeast consists of the fertile mesopotamic zone and the Chaco plains, whose dense quebracho forests are the major source of the tannin used in leather tanning. On the Argentine-Brazil border, in the far northeast of the maté-producing Province of Misiones, are the magnificent Iguassú Falls.

The Pampas, the heart of Argentina, are situated south of the Chaco. This great plain is divided into roughly five production areas: milk, fruit, and vegetables around Buenos Aires; livestock from Entre Rios to Bahía Blanca; corn and flax around Rosario; alfalfa in the west and south; and the famous "wheat crescent zone," which extends about six hundred miles.

In the western Andean mountain area, the site of Mt. Aconcagua, the highest peak in the Hemisphere, there are temperate and luxuriant valleys, extensive salt plains, and arid tablelands. Grapes, olives, and citrus fruit are cultivated in sunlit valleys surrounded by the snow-covered Andes, and strung along the foot of the mountains is a magnificent lake region surrounded by heavily forested national parks.

South of the Colorado River is the plateau of Patagonia, arid and windy, devoted mainly to raising sheep and producing wool. The most important oil field is at Comodoro Rivadavia, in Patagonia.

Tierra del Fuego, an island lying south of the Strait of Megellan, is owned by both Chile and Argentina. Ushuaia, capital of the Argentine sector, is the southernmost seat of organized government in the world.

Some nine million Argentines, more than one third of the total population, live in Greater Buenos Aires, a vast urban complex where the country's government and a significant part of its political, commercial, and financial activities are concentrated. Its busy port is one of the largest in the world.

Rosario is the second city of the republic, noted for its modernity and for its river port used to export grains and other agricultural commodities. It is also a major industrial and commercial center.

The influence of Spanish culture is still apparent in the colonial cities of the northwest: in Córdoba, with its tradition of learning; in Tucumán, known as the "garden of the republic"; in historic Salta; and in beautiful Mendoza, headquarters of the wine-making industry.

**History.** In 1516 Juan Díaz de Solís, seeking a route to the "western sea," anchored in the great estuary later called the River Plate and took possession of these lands in the name of the Spanish Crown. Tales of the fabulous riches of the Inca empire inspired expeditions by other conquistadors and adventurers, but it was not until 1580 that Juan de Garay was able to found the city of Buenos Aires on a permanent basis, an undertaking in which Pedro de Mendoza had failed in 1536.

During the first two centuries Argentine territory was of little importance to Spain, and not until 1776 was the Viceroyalty of the River Plate established, with Buenos Aires as its capital. Shortly thereafter, its port was opened to trade with Spain and other nations and the prosperity of the colony was assured.

On May 25, 1810, the people demanded their own government, forced the Viceroy to resign, and set up a board of patriots known as the "First Junta."

The national hero, José de San Martin, after winning freedom for Argentina, continued the struggle on the other side of the Andes to obtain the freedom of the peoples of Chile and Peru. On July 9, 1816, the Congress of Tucumán proclaimed the Declaration of National Independence. Argentina experienced decades of instability while the Unitary Party, bent on central control, quarreled with the Federalists, who insisted on local autonomy. In 1853, the Congress of Santa Fe adopted the federal constitution, which united the country and marked the beginning of the modern republican period.

Building on the original population core of Spanish descent, a steady wave of European immigrants, mostly Italian but including as well large groups of Spaniards, English, Germans, French, Jews, and Arabs, gradually shaped the present-day nation of Argentina.

The first period of the Argentine **caudillismo** ended with the presidencies of two great statesmen, Bartolomé Mitre and Domingo Faustino Sarmiento. This was the beginning of the evolution of a national identity. In 1912, a more liberal democratic and representative organization was introduced, as a result of the struggles of the popular leader Hipólito Irigoyen, who in 1916 became chief of state. Social reforms and rapid industrial expansion characterized the ensuing years, despite political struggles between radicals and conservatives. In 1946, Juan Domingo Perón, a military officer, was elected President with the support of the Labor Party. Perón remained in power until his overthrow by the army in 1955. Arturo Frondizi was the first popularly elected President after the downfall of Peronism. Gen. Roberto M. Levingston assumed control of the government in 1970.

**Culture.** Although the total Indian population of Argentina probably never exceeded a half million, the more warlike tribes stoutly resisted the Spaniards; in southern Argentina they continued to be a serious obstacle to the settlement and development of the country as late as the 1800's, when the last was finally subdued. Today, some descendants of the Quechuas dwell in the northwestern highlands adjoining Bolivia; remnants of the Guaraní nation are found in the northeast; while small numbers of Araucanians and Patagonians live in western Patagonia.

Religious art and architecture were the greatest cultural heritage from the colonial era. Fortunately for Argentina, its most outstanding statesmen were also noted men of ideas and letters. President Sarmiento was the author of works on sociology, education, and history, as were Bartolomé Mitre and Juan Bautista Alberdi. The first of the great Argentine poets and writers of the nineteenth century was Esteban Echeverría. Gaucho literature reached its highest expression in the epic poem **Martín Fierro,** by José Hernández. Among the finest Argentine philosophers and essayists were José Ingenieros and Alejandro Korn, and today, Victoria Ocampo, Jorge Luis Borges, and José Luis (Francisco) Romero. In poetry Leopoldo Lugones and Alfonsina Storni stand out. Argentine letters abound in excellent prose writers such as Ricardo Güiraldes, the author of **Don Segundo Sombra,** and recently, Leopoldo Marechal and Julio Cortázar. Argentine scientists have been awarded the Nobel Prize on two occasions, and Carlos Saavedra Lamas won the Peace Prize in 1936. Since the time of the genre painter Prilidiano Pueyrredón (1823-1870), Argentina has produced a number of outstanding painters, sculptors, and sketchers. Today, Argentina is one of the Latin American countries in which artistic development has reached its highest point. Throughout the republic, there are some ninety-eight museums under the auspices of the national government. The modern art movement began about the time of World War I and has grown steadily. Among the country's many outstanding painters of the twentieth century are S. Eugenio Daneri, Emilio Pettoruti, Raquel Forner, Antonio Berni. The same is true of Argentine music, which has such composers as José Castro and Alberto Ginastera, and one of the finest opera houses in the world, the Colón Theater of Buenos Aires.

The most typical song of the pampa is the **estilo,** always dealing with life on the plains, and the most typical dances are the **zamba** and the **gato.** The **refalosa, triste,** and **vidalita,** also common in Peru and Chile, are still danced in the northern and western provinces. The distinctive Argentine tango is popular throughout America and in Europe.

**Economy.** The major components of Argentina's GNP are trades and services (43 per cent), industry (35 per cent), and agriculture (16 per cent). Domestic industry can satisfy most of the nation's needs, including automobiles, machinery, and appliances. Grain, meat, wool, and manufactures are the principal exports.

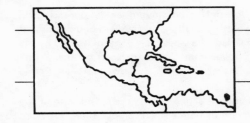

**BARBADOS**
Population: 300,000

BARBADOS, KNOWN AS "the Little England of the tropics," is the eastern-most of the Windward Islands, which form the southern curve of the Lesser Antilles in the Caribbean. It is the only one of the Antilles never subject to Spanish or French rule, having belonged exclusively to England from the time of its colonization in 1627 until it became a sovereign nation in November 1966.

**Geography.** Pear-shaped Barbados measures only twenty miles long by fourteen wide. It is the most densely populated country in the Western Hemisphere, with more than 1,500 persons per square mile. In general, the land is level, with low outcroppings of limestone. There is very little natural vegetation and virtually no grasslands or woods, with the exception of the forest covering the heights of Mount Hillaby. The southern part of the island has many sugar cane plantations.

The island obtains its water supply from limestone deposits and springs, but its rivers are few and none of them is navigable. Although Barbados has no natural ports—Carlisle is an open anchorage with a protected inner bay— there is a new deep-draft artificial harbor west of Bridgetown. The serene, transparent sea and the silver sands of the west coast rival in beauty the beaches of the southeast coast, sheltered by coral banks that extend out to sea for nearly three miles. Flying fish are a special attraction of these beaches. The climate of Barbados is healthful, with no abrupt changes in the weather. The humidity is tempered by the northeast trade winds, which blow constantly. The island's capital and major population center is picturesque Bridgetown.

**History.** Up to the sixteenth century Barbados contained Arawak communities, but those had disappeared prior to the arrival of the first English ship in 1625. During the next three years British companies established two colonies. Sir William Courteen founded Jamestown in honor of King James I; its name was later changed to Holetown. The second colony, St. Michael's Town, founded by the Earl of Carlisle, is today the city of Bridgetown. From the beginning, the inhabitants of Barbados claimed the rights and privileges enjoyed by the English overseas. In 1627 the post of governor and a council and an assembly were set up to govern the colony. Since 1639, when the Parliament of Barbados met for the first time, the system of representative government has prevailed continuously. Barbados obtained its independence and became a sovereign nation on November 30, 1966. It is a member of the British Commonwealth of Nations. Its system of government is a parliamentary democracy, headed by a Governor General named by the British Crown. The functions of government are exercised by the Prime Minister and the Cabinet of Ministers. Errol W. Barrow has been Prime Minister since independence.

**Culture.** Barbados can be proud of its literacy rate (98 per cent, one of the highest in the world), and its system of universal free education, to which nearly 20 per cent of the annual national budget is allotted. The country's natives, or Bajans, as they call themselves, are charming, hospitable, gay, and ingenious. Their independent spirit and zeal for learning are legendary. Cricket is the national sport. Prominent Bajan authors include George Lamming and Austin Clarke. Carl Brook Hagen is a noted sculptor. The Barbados Museum is one of the finest in the West Indies.

**Economy.** Sugar is the chief crop and sugar processing the chief industry, followed by tourism. Edible oils, lard, margarine, rum, and soap are produced.

**BOLIVIA**
Population: 4.8 million

LOCATED IN THE VERY heart of the South American continent, the nation that proudly bears the name of the Liberator is basically an Andean country, despite the fact that its territory encompasses a vast tropical zone. The Bolivian altiplano, more than twelve thousand feet above sea level, was the cradle of the country's pre-Columbian civilizations and is still today the site of its major cities and the geographic factor most strongly influencing the Bolivians' life style.

**Geography.** Bolivia has no outlet of its own to the sea. Snow-covered mountains of incomparable beauty rise from the altiplano, an area extraordinarily rich in mineral resources, buffeted by frequent cold winds and sectioned off in some places by defiles and gorges. The intermediate zone, known as the **Yungas,** consists of an extensive series of ravines. The Department of Cochabamba, because of its fertile soil, is known as the garden and breadbasket of Bolivia. In the east are the tropical lowlands, underdeveloped and underpopulated lands used mainly for grazing and ranching.

Illampú, Illimani, and Sajama, three of the highest mountains in America (over twenty thousand feet), are located in Bolivian territory, while Lake Titicaca, at 12,500 feet above sea level the world's highest navigable body of water, lies partly in Bolivia and partly in Peru.

La Paz, one of the world's highest cities, set in a great notch in the sierra, is the seat of government and center of the country's political and economic life, although the constitutional capital of the republic is the city of Sucre. Cochabamba, in the midst of Bolivia's farming zone, has the second largest population. Potosí, at 13,340 feet, a museum city famous for the wealth of its silver mines since the early years of the conquest, is at the foot of the famous Cerro Rico (Rich Hill). Oruro, the tin center; Santa Cruz, center of a petroleum-producing area; Sorata, a favorite with mountain climbers; and Copacabana, on the shores of picturesque Lake Titicaca, are also noteworthy.

**History.** The Lake Titicaca region had once been the setting of the great Tiahuanaco culture, but the Inca Empire controlled the vast altiplano when the Spaniards arrived. During the decade from 1530 to 1540, the conquistador Francisco Pizarro sent expeditionary forces from Peru into Bolivia. In 1539 Pedro Anzures de Campo Redondo founded the city of La Plata, known as the city of four names, since it was successively called Charcas, Chuquisaca, and, finally, Sucre in honor of its liberator. The discovery of silver in Potosí enhanced the importance of the Bolivian territory in Spanish eyes. In 1559, what is now Bolivia became the Audiencia of Charcas, part of the Viceroyalty of Peru, and was known as Upper Peru, but in 1776 it was transferred to the new Viceroyalty of the River Plate. Independence movements began early in the nineteenth century. Upper Peru was the first Spanish colony in America to assert its right to independence, by deposing the president of the Audiencia in Chuquisaca in 1809. The same year the people of La Paz also overthrew the Spanish authorities, following the leadership of Pedro Domingo Murillo, but the revolt ended in failure and Murillo was condemned to death.

The country officially proclaimed its independence in 1825. After his victory at Ayacucho, in Peru, General Antonio José de Sucre liberated the colony from Spanish rule and Simón Bolívar drafted the Constitution of the new republic, which took its present name in his honor. General Sucre became President in December 1826. In 1836, the country formed a confederation with Peru, which lasted only four years. The War of the Pacific (1879-1883), in which Bolivia and Peru joined forces against Chile, originated in a series of differences with Chile over the Atacama coast and its rich nitrate deposits, then belonging to Bolivia. As a result of that war Bolivia lost its coast on the Pacific and has been a landlocked country ever since. In 1932, Bolivia was involved in the Chaco War with Paraguay over possession of the Chaco Boreal, an undeveloped plains area located in the center of South America. Hostilities ceased in 1935, and in 1938 the boundary between the two countries was drawn and a treaty signed.

A revolution in 1952, backed by a popular reform movement, led to the nationalization of tin mines and improved social legislation. In 1970 Gen. Juan José Torres assumed the presidency.

**Culture.** The two factors of the Bolivian cultural complex, Indian and Spanish, exerted a mutual influence and shared in the development of the nation. The Indian, predominant in the population, includes two main groups, the Quechuas and Aymaras. For its part, the Spanish component is illustrated by the excellent architecture of the old colonial cities and their rich imagery, as well as their many other pieces of art. Spanish traditions and customs are still preserved in Potosí and Sucre, as in other towns with strong Indian traits, such as Copacabana, site of the sanctuary of the Virgin of Copacabana.

Potosí, particularly, was the focus of the colony's cultural life during the sixteenth century because of its mining wealth and urban development. Charcas (Sucre) was the seat of the very early University of San Francisco Javier, considered as the cradle of independence of the Hemisphere, founded in 1624. The country's isolation did not prevent the evolution of cultural activities and the flourishing of arts and letters. Gabriel René Moreno is, perhaps, the most notable literary figure of nineteenth century Bolivia, and the novelist Nataniel Aguirre was also prominent then. Earlier in the present century, Ricardo Jaimes Freyre and Alcides Argüedas were important in Bolivian letters, and, more recently, Fernando Diez de Medina.

Bolivian folk expression is one of the richest and most attractive in the Hemisphere. The tone of its music is gay in the valleys and melancholic on the altiplano. Crafts reach an incomparable level of originality and charm in the ritual and carnival masks.

**Economy.** Tin continues to be the mainstay of Bolivia's economy, but petroleum and natural gas are becoming increasingly important. Agriculture accounts for 23 per cent of GNP, mining and petroleum 17 per cent. Major crops are potatoes, sorghum, corn, sugar, and coffee.

**BRAZIL**
Population: 95.3 million

LARGEST OF THE LATIN AMERICAN nations and fifth largest in the world, Portuguese-speaking Brazil occupies one half of the South American continent. The splendor of its colonial monuments stands in contrast to its ultra-modern cities and growing industrial might.

**Geography.** Brazil's climate ranges from tropical to temperate. The Amazon River, the largest on earth, runs across the entire country from west to east, contributing to the typical jungle profile of the vast area drained by its many tributaries. Roraima Federal Territory and the states of Amazonas, Pará, and Mato Grosso, largely untouched, contrast dramatically with the other parts of the national territory. In the states of Rio Grande do Sul, Paraná, Minas Gerais, and São Paulo industry is well developed and the highest levels of civilization and progress are found. On the other hand, the Brazilian Northeast has its own distinctive climatic features and life-style. Enormous plains predominate in the low central plateau and the lowlands along the coastal strip, and in the particularly humid Amazon River basin. In the more temperate far south, where land is fertile, great **fazendas** produce coffee, cotton, fruits, and livestock. The area is also the location of the largest ore deposits currently mined, and of the famous Iguassú Falls which Brazil shares with Argentina.

Only a short distance from the coast, along which Brazilian culture has developed, are all the great cities of the country, except for its capital, Brasília, with its fine examples of contemporary architecture. From south to north they are: Pôrto Alegre; São Paulo, the most highly industrialized city in Latin America and one of the most progressive in the world; Rio de Janeiro, with its incomparable scenic beauty; Salvador de Bahia, of ancient tradition; Recife (Pernambuco), Natal, Fortaleza (Ceara), and Belem (Para). Ouro Prêto, a museum city, preserves the splendor of colonial times. But Brazil is today moving toward the conquest of what was only yesterday a vast unexplored hinterland.

**History.** Brazil was discovered in 1500 by the Portuguese navigator Pedro Alvares Cabral, who claimed it for the Portuguese crown. Cabral called the region Vera Cruz. Portuguese colonization was mainly on the coast, and the heart of the region remained unexplored until a conquistador in the service of Pizarro, Francisco Orellana, starting from the Spanish side of the continent, set out on a fantastic adventure, traveling down the Amazon to its mouth. In 1549, the government of the region was unified and its capital set up in Salvador (Bahia), where it remained until 1763. The first independence movement, in 1789, was led by the idealist Joaquim José da Silva Xavier, more commonly known as Tiradentes (Toothpuller).

In 1815, Brazil was elevated to the rank of kingdom. Dom Pedro was appointed regent of Brazil in 1821. On September 7, 1822, Pedro I declared the independence of Brazil and, after being proclaimed Constitutional Emperor, named as Prime Minister José Bonifácio de Andrada e Silva, national hero and Patriarch of Independence. The emergence of a republican spirit over the next fifty years brought the abolition of slavery in 1888 and the end of the monarchy. In November 1889, the republic was proclaimed without bloodshed. Its official name today is the Federal Republic of Brazil.

The great political and economic centers of the country, Rio de Janeiro and São Paulo, have been rivals during the republican period. As a result of the 1929 economic crisis, Getulio Vargas came into power, and his strong personality exercised a decisive influence on Brazilian political life until he left office in 1945. Five years later, Vargas was reelected, and in 1954 the nation was stirred by his suicide. Two principal events marked the term of office of his successor, President Juscelino Kubitschek. Nationally, there was the beginning of the new capital, Brasília, which became the seat of government in 1960; on the inter-American level, there was Operation Pan America, the forerunner of the Alliance for Progress. Despite economic and political difficulties, the succeeding governments have pledged themselves to further the social progress and development of the great Brazilian nation. Emílio Garrastazu Médici succeeded Artur da Costa e Silva as President in 1969.

**Culture.** Brazil's native population was scant and divided into a number of tribes, factors that favored establishment of the European colonies. But the great shortage of workers made it necessary to import them from Africa, which marked the beginning of slavery and the consequent contribution of the African factor to the ethnic complex of contemporary Brazil. Other European and Asiatic immigrations have helped to give the country its rich cultural diversity. Brazil preserves an indelible Portuguese stamp in architecture and art, of which the historical sites of Ouro Prêto and Pelourinho, in Bahia, are excellent examples.

Brazilian thought and literature began to evolve in the early years of the colonial period, proliferated under the influence of romanticism, with José de Alencar, and developed in the middle of the nineteenth century into a naturalistic and realistic movement led by Aluísio de Azevedo and Machado de Assis. Euclides da Cunha, Graça Aranha, and Joaquim Nabuco have been translated into several languages, while the contemporary sociologist

Gilberto Freyre has contributed more fully than any of his predecessors to the scientific understanding of Brazil as a nation. Among the most outstanding contemporary novelists, mention should be made of Erico Veríssimo and Jorge Amado, and among the large number of essayists, Alceu Amoroso Lima. If in the field of classical music Brazil can be proud of such distinguished composers as Carlos Gomes and Heitor Villa-Lobos, in the popular vein the country has one of the most varied and extensive repertoires in the Hemisphere.

Brazilian contemporary architecture is famous throughout the world. Oscar Niemeyer and Lucio Costa were the builders of Brasília. The name of Cândido Portinari is internationally included among the great muralists.

Among contemporary painters, pioneers of the modern movement in Brazil, are Emiliano di Cavalcanti, Tarsila do Amaral, and the late Alberto da Veiga Guignard. In other fields, the following have achieved recognition: the engraver Roberto de Lamonica; the draftsman Marcelo Grassman; and the sculptors Lygia Clark, Mário Cravo, and Bruno Giorgi.

Brazil has a rich variety of folk arts and customs, the result of its ethnic composition and its vast and diverse land. The music of the Northeast, like the handicrafts, reflects the African heritage. Carnival is celebrated throughout Brazil, but is most spectacular in Rio de Janeiro, with samba music and **marchinhas**.

**Economy.** Large-scale industrialization in recent years has diversified Brazil's economy to the point that manufacturing accounts for one-fourth of GNP and occupies more than half the labor force. Coffee continues to be the principal export, followed by manufactured products, iron ore, and cacao.

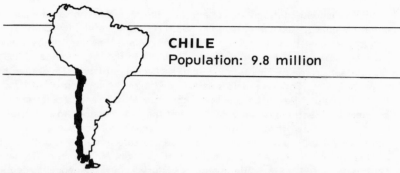

# CHILE
## Population: 9.8 million

CHILE, LAND OF spectacular scenery and world-famous wines, has achieved an advanced stage of development, a high level of learning, and an exemplary democratic evolution.

**Geography.** Chile extends almost 2,700 miles to the southernmost tip of South America. This narrow ribbon of land (nowhere more than 250 miles wide) lies imprisoned between the snow-capped Andean ranges and the Pacific. Under its northern Atacama Desert are the world's largest deposits of nitrate. In this desert region are places in which no rain has ever been recorded. Antofagasta is the major port of the nitrate coast.

Central Chile, from Coquimbo to Concepción, contains the bulk of the population, the major cities, the largest and richest farms, and the industrial centers of the country. The Andean ranges, rich in gold, silver, copper, nickel, lead, manganese, and other minerals, reach heights exceeding 21,000 feet between Copiapó and Santiago.

The Chilean lake region, one of South America's most popular resort and tourist areas, extends north of Puerto Montt. From there south, a maze of channels and islands makes coastal navigation dangerous. Steamers end their run at Punta Arenas, a busy modern port on the Strait of Magellan and Chile's southernmost city. As the center of a vast sheep-raising industry, Punta Arenas is the shipping port for wool and mutton; and more recently crude oil and coal. Patagonia, one of the world's finest sheep-raising regions, is a land of virgin forests, strong winds, snow-capped volcanic cones, sparkling lakes, glaciers, and fjords. South of the Strait of Magellan lies the group of islands known as Tierra del Fuego, shared by Chile and Argentina. The rugged islands support a huge population of sheep. Chile's possessions in the Pacific include Easter Island and the Juan Fernández Islands, and its territory extends southward into the frozen Antarctic.

Santiago, capital of the republic, is the political, economic, and artistic center of the nation. Valparaíso, the first port and second city of Chile, is one of the major seaports on the west coast of South America. Viña del Mar, with its renowned casino, is a famous seaside resort.

**History.** Northern Chile formed part of the Inca Empire at the time of its conquest by Francisco Pizarro and his partner Diego de Almagro. Pedro de

Valdivia founded Santiago in 1541 and laid the foundation of a new colony. Colonization was slow because of the fierce resistance of the freedom-loving Araucanians, led by Lautaro and Caupolicán, whose superior numbers wore down the Spanish army and defeated Valdivia in the last months of 1553.

Chileans remained loyal to the Spanish Crown until 1810. On September 18 of that year, Chilean patriots established a self-governing junta. Under the leadership of Bernardo O'Higgins and José M. Carrera, a congress was convoked in Santiago on July 4, 1811, and the first republican constitution was adopted. Spanish royalist forces from Peru regained possession of the country; but Chile was liberated from Spanish rule in decisive battles won by the Army of the Andes, led by José de San Martin and Bernardo O'Higgins, in 1817-1818. Chile began its history as an independent republic with O'Higgins, honored as the "father of his country," as supreme director.

Following the border war with Bolivia and Peru, 1879-83, the country secured prosperous territories in the far north, while the twentieth century ushered in a process of industrial development and social reforms which, despite successive economic crises, produced a steadily rising trend in the national economy. From the institutional and political standpoints, Chile has been characterized by maintenance of a system of democratic order and traditional respect for constitutional standards. A strong shift to the left was revealed by the victory of the Christian Democratic Party in 1964 and the recent election of President Salvador Allende.

**Culture.** The prolonged and bloody struggle required to subdue the Araucanian Indians was recorded for all time by a Spanish captain, Alonso de Ercilla, who described its most heroic episodes in an immortal poem, **La Araucana.** But the true origin of Chilean literature can be traced to the very beginnings of national independence, when the reorganization of education and the expansion of school facilities became the primary concern of O'Higgins and other founders and reformers. In 1842, the old University of San Felipe was reorganized as the University of Chile with Andrés Bello as its rector, and at the same time an intellectual movement began to evolve, strengthened by a wave of European immigration, which was to develop outstanding men in all of the scientific, literary, and artistic fields. Naturalists like Carlos Emilio Paster and historians and essayists like Miguel Luis Amunátegui, Benjamín Vicuña Mackenna, José Toribio Medina, and José Victorino Lastarria flourished during the second half of the last century. Successive generations of literary figures included Pedro Prado; Gabriela Mistral, winner of the Nobel Prize for literature; and Pablo Neruda. Chilean artists of great distinction range from Pedro Lira, the great innovator, to the avant garde painter Roberto Matta.

Classical music was developed by such renowned composers as Domingo Santa Cruz and such internationally known interpreters as Claudio Arrau.

Most of the folk arts in Chile reflect its Spanish tradition. The native strain, a very minor component in the current population, which is strongly European in origin, has had little influence on the culture as a whole. The best known popular dance is the **cueca.**

**Economy.** Industry is now the leading sector of the Chilean economy, contributing about 25 per cent to the GNP. Wholesale and retail trade accounts for 21 per cent, mining for 11 per cent, and agriculture for 10 per cent. Copper and copper products head the list of exports, followed by iron ore, fishmeal, nitrates, and newsprint.

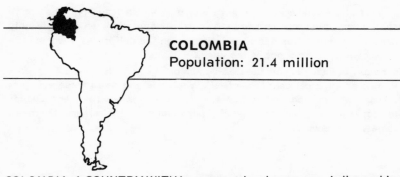

**COLOMBIA**
Population: 21.4 million

COLOMBIA, A COUNTRY WITH immense natural resources, is the ranking producer of gold in Latin America, the major world source of emeralds, and one of the few producers of platinum. It follows Brazil as the second largest coffee grower in the world.

**Geography.** The country comprises coastal lowlands on both the Caribbean and the Pacific; from south to north three parallel spurs of the Andes traverse the western half of the country, forming broad plateaus and valleys; and the eastern zone is made up of plains in the northern part and vast stretches of the Orinoco and Amazon basins. The principal rivers are the Cauca and the Magdalena.

Bogotá, the capital, is located at 8,700 feet on a plateau of the eastern cordillera. It projects the essence of national cultural traditions, conserving its characteristic colonial architecture side by side with tall modern buildings. Medellín, the second largest city in the country, is an intellectual, industrial, and commercial center of great importance, as well as the center of a coffee-growing zone famous for the quality of its harvest. Cali, in the luxuriant Cauca Valley, is the Colombian city that has recorded the greatest and most rapid agricultural and industrial development. Popáyan, the birthplace of many distinguished men, conserves priceless treasures of colonial art and architecture. Cartagena, strategically situated beside one of the loveliest bays in the Caribbean, was ranked among the richest and most active colonial commercial centers. Bucaramanga is another large coffee and tobacco producer. Barranquilla, a tropical city and maritime and river port, is a major embarkation point. Manizales, Pereira, and Armenia are progressive industrial cities in the eastern part of Colombia. Cúcuta, located in a highly prosperous farming and ranching zone, owes its development primarily to its proximity to the Catatumbo oil fields and the Venezuelan border. Colombia's principal port on the Pacific is Buenaventura. Santa Marta, on the Caribbean, is one of the oldest cities in South America.

**History.** Colombia, the only country whose name honors the great discoverer, was not discovered by Columbus at all but by Alonso de Ojeda, who accompanied him on his second voyage to the New World. Between 1500, when Colombia was discovered, and 1538, when Gonzalo Jiménez de

Quesada founded Santa Fe de Bogotá, the territory was widely explored and the first colonizers settled. Jiménez de Quesada, the illustrious marshal and symbol of justice, dominated the first forty years of New Granada. Despite frequent attacks by filibusters, French, English, and Dutch, the colony prospered and was raised to the status of a viceroyalty in 1717. Growing restlessness and a spirit of rebellion among creoles of the upper class, as well as among the people, culminated in the Revolution of the **Comuneros** in 1781. The independence movement was further encouraged by the great patriot and intellectual leader Antonio Nariño, who translated the French **Declaration of the Rights of Man** into Spanish. On July 20, 1810, the creoles, eager for a government of their own, established the Supreme Junta of the Kingdom of New Granada. On July 16, 1813, independence was proclaimed, but Spain recaptured New Granada and restored the viceroyalty. In 1819, Simón Bolívar and Francisco de Paula Santander, at the head of their armies, left Venezuela to cross the Andes and win a decisive victory over the Spaniards at Boyacá. Bolívar's dream of seeing New Granada and Venezuela united to form Gran Colombia was realized at the Congress of Angostura. Ecuador joined these countries in 1822. But the federation was dissolved in 1830 when Venezuela and Ecuador resolved to become sovereign states. In 1832, a new Colombian constitution established the federal form of government. General Santander, known as the "Man of Law," was the first President.

The 1885 revolution put an end to the federal system, and since 1886 Colombia has been a unitary of centralized republic.

The rival Conservative and Liberal political parties have consistently opposed each other, and occasionally staged violent confrontations, in their pursuit of public power throughout the gradual evolution of the long republican process. At the end of the nineteenth century, civil strife resulted in many deaths. In 1930, the Conservative Party leaders who had governed the country for many years were succeeded by the Liberal Enrique Olaya Herrera, the first in a series of Liberal presidents that continued until the election of Conservative Mariano Ospina Pérez in 1946. The assassination of the leftist leader Jorge Eliecer Gaitan in 1948 touched off a mass uprising known as the **bogotazo.** The new Conservative era was ended by the overthrow of Laureano Gómez and the rise to power of General Gustavo Rojas Pinilla, who served until 1957. Under the terms of a parity pact, Liberals and Conservatives now take turns in governing the country, a policy of harmonious understanding initiated by President Alberto Lleras Camargo. Misael Pastrana was elected President in 1970.

**Culture.** The plateau and the coast represent very different values in the Colombian cultural complex. Cartagena and Barranquilla share the characteristics of the Caribbean peoples, as well as their ethnic composition. The Negro influence is particularly apparent in their popular music. In contrast, Bogotá and the Andean communities, basically Indian in makeup, maintain a way of life and exhibit aesthetic tastes peculiar to that region. The Spanish tradition of the old viceroyalty is evident in the architecture of its major cities, rich in monuments of historical and artistic interest, while Colombian archaeology can point with pride to the Quimbaya, Chibcha, and Chiriqui cultures, and the impressive sculptures at San Agustín.

From the founding of the first print shop during the viceroyalty in 1737 to the present, successive generations of writers, poets, and essayists have made their contributions to Colombian literature. Such masters of the language as Miguel Antonio Caro and poets and writers like Julio Arboleda, Porfirio Barba Jacob, José Asunción Silva, José Eustasio Rivera, Jorge Isaac, and Guillermo Valencia bring honor to Colombia. The Caro y Cuervo Institute, a sanctuary of the Spanish language, is named for Antonio Caro and Rufino José Cuervo, author of the essay "Critique of the Bogotanian Language." Distinguished nineteenth century historians include José Manuel Restrepo. Contemporary Colombian figures in literature and the arts are a legitimate source of pride for the Hemisphere, among them such eminent novelists as Gabriel García Márquez and essayists of the stature of Germán Arciniegas.

**Economy.** About 30 per cent of Colombia's GNP comes from agriculture, and 20 per cent from industry. Industries include textiles, beverages, petroleum, iron and steel, metal working, and food processing. Coffee, petroleum, and cotton are the principal exports.

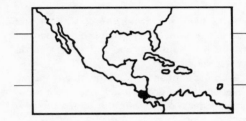

**COSTA RICA**
Population: 1.8 million

ONE OF THE SMALLEST of the Latin American republics in area and population, Costa Rica is famous throughout the Hemisphere for its strong tradition of order and democracy and for its advanced system of public education.

**Geography.** Three volcanic mountain ranges of different heights cross the territory of Costa Rica and provide it with a variety of climates despite its tropical location. The hot lowlands along the Caribbean coast with their abundant rainfall are excellent for growing bananas and cacao, while coffee is cultivated in the colder regions. The vast forest areas have not been intensively developed. The heart of the country is the central plateau—with its lovely prairies, picturesque villages, and untouched woodlands—where most of the country's population is concentrated and the best crops are produced. The climate on the plateau is mild and pleasant and its soil is extremely fertile because of the volcanic deposits accumulated for centuries. Irazú is the highest and most active of the nine volcanoes in Costa Rica, while Poás can be seen to give off smoke intermittently. In March 1963 Irazú, which had been inactive since 1920, began to spew tons of ashes over the entire central valley; the ashfall continued for nearly two years. The Poás crater measures more than a mile across. On a clear day the Caribbean Sea and the Pacific Ocean can be seen from its crest.

San José, the country's capital, is the center of commercial and cultural activity. Other important cities are Alajuela, the center of an important sugar district; Cartago, the oldest city in the country, where the Central American Court of Justice functioned from 1907 to 1918; Heredia, famous for its flowers and intensive ranching activity; Puntarenas, the main Pacific seaport; and Puerto Limón, on the Caribbean coast.

**History.** The pre-Columbian Indians who lived in what is today the territory of Costa Rica were the Chorotega and the Boruca, among others; they were excellent craftsmen, as evidenced by the many ceramic pieces unearthed and now on exhibit in museums throughout the world. They were also skilled in the art of goldsmithing and the use of jade. Although Columbus sailed along the country's coasts and his brother explored the interior, Costa Rica's real history did not begin until 1564, with the founding of Cartago by Juan Vázquez de Coronado and the settlement of the first Basque colonists. He envisioned that fertile land peopled by peaceful homesteaders, and carried out his dream by bringing fifty families from the provinces of Galicia and Aragon in Spain to the salubrious central plateau. He also brought horses, cattle, and swine to Costa Rica, and it is said that one of the first cattle ranches in the New World was established there.

In line with the spirit of the era, on September 15, 1821, the independence of the Spanish colonies of Central America was proclaimed, and Costa Rica, which formed part of the Captaincy General of Guatemala, joined the new Federation of the United Provinces of Central America. When the Federation threatened to break apart, the country proclaimed its own Constitution and became independent. William Walker, a U.S. adventurer, tried to take over the region shortly afterwards, but was defeated by the resolve and patriotism of the national hero, President Juan Rafael Mora.

During the last quarter of the nineteenth century the country enjoyed orderly democratic development and increased prosperity. Since 1948 the army of this small and exemplary nation has been abolished and the responsibility for public order placed in the care of a small police force. José Figueres was reelected President in 1970.

**Culture.** The commitment to democracy has favored the evolution of intellectual activity and the attainment of high levels of public education. Novelists, poets and writers such as Manuel González Zeledón, Aquileo J. Echeverría, Alfredo Cardona Peña, and Fabián Dobles, among others, exemplify the country's literature, which also includes enchanting tales typical of a national folklore that differs from the rest of Central America because most of the population is of European descent. The famous Costa Rican carts, with their bright colors and original designs, are a good example of the folk art. The pre-Columbian heritage is notable.

**Economy.** About 24 per cent of Costa Rica's GNP comes from agriculture, forestry, and fishing; about 18 per cent from manufacturing and mining. Gold, manganese, and sulphur are the principal minerals. Costa Rica exports coffee, bananas, cattle, meat, cacao, and sugar. The nation's industries include fiberglass, aluminum, fertilizer, roofing, and cement.

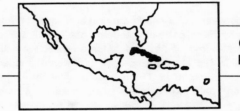

**CUBA**
Population: 8.4 million

THE LARGEST ISLAND in the Antilles, Cuba occupies a strategic geographic position at the entrance to the Gulf of Mexico. It was the last of the New World republics to win its independence from Spain.

**Geography.** Approximately half the island is plain or rolling, and the remainder is mountainous. The highest mountains are in the Sierra Maestra, on the eastern end of the island.

The deep, well-formed bays along the coasts provide excellent ports. The island is surrounded by innumerable bays and islets, the largest of which is the beautiful Isle of Pines, famous for its fruit and marble. Havana, the principal city of the Antilles and the historic capital of Cuba, is a mixture of native and cosmopolitan, ancient and modern tradition. The imposing fortresses that surround the city are evidence of its strategic importance and status as a stronghold during the centuries of colonial rule.

At the far eastern end of the island stands the second largest city in the country, Santiago de Cuba. The famous Bellamar Caves are not far from the city of Matanzas, capital of the province of the same name. More than a hundred large sugar mills scattered throughout the island serve as centers of industrial and agricultural activity, helping to raise living standards and improve communications facilities in rural areas.

**History.** Cuba was discovered by Columbus in 1492 and explored and settled by Diego Velázquez in 1515. The sparse Indian population was peace loving and soon died out completely. The island prospered as the center of the routes to the Indies, attracting many pirates, who infested its coasts during the sixteenth and seventeenth centuries. Spain's war with England provoked the siege and capture of Havana by the English in 1762. The city shortly returned to Spanish hands in exchange for the cession of Florida to England. The richest and most prosperous of Spanish colonies during the nineteenth century, the Captaincy General of Cuba based its economy primarily on sugar, coffee, and tobacco.

Several insurrections led to the Ten-year War, which began in 1868 when Carlos Manuel de Céspedes launched the Proclamation of Independence known as the Cry of Yara. This was followed by a brief interval of peace as a result of the Pact of Zanjón between Cuba and Spain, but soon again the in-dependentist spirit, directed by the apostle of freedom José Martí, stirred the country to war. Generals Máximo Gómez and Antonio Maceo were the great heroes of this unprecedented struggle against a powerful modern army of three hundred thousand Spaniards. The intervention of the United States, which declared war on Spain in behalf of its Cuban allies, precipi-tated the liberation of Cuba.

The first President of the new united Republic was Tomás Estrada Palma, who took office on May 20, 1902. Despite the political conflicts that characterized the progress of republican Cuba, economic and social de-velopment raised the country to one of the highest levels in America. Ful-gencio Batista was the dominant figure in Cuban politics from 1934 to 1959. In January 1959 Fidel Castro swept to power at the head of an apparently democratic movement and carried out a communist revolution that brought the country into the sphere of influence of the Soviet Union. Owing to this fact and to Cuba's intervention in the internal affairs of other American repub-lics, the Eighth Meeting of Consultation of Ministers of Foreign Affairs ex-cluded the Government of Cuba from participation in the organs and activi-ties of the OAS.

**Culture.** Cuba's connection with Spain influenced its cultural evolution up to the beginning of the present century. There are many beautiful examples of colonial art and architecture. The University of Havana, founded in 1704, and the Economic Society of Friends of the Country helped to form a legion of thinkers and writers of first rank, such as Félix Varela, Felipe Poey and Antonio Saco. Cuban poetry contributed to Spanish letters such famous names as José María de Heredia, Gertrudis Gómez de Avellaneda, and Cirilo Villaverde. Toward the end of nineteenth century, when a national identity began to take shape, the country achieved its finest intellectual flowering, as expressed by the philosopher Enrique José Varona, Rafael Montoro, Enrique Piñeiro, Julian del Casal, and José Martí himself, the thinker and poet who was the forerunner of the Modernist movement in the Americas. A Cuban scientist, Carlos Finlay, made a decisive contribution to the eradication of yellow fever by discovering its vector.

During the republican stage there was an expansion of cultural institu-tions and an increase in literary and artistic activity in which many Cubans, including Antonio Sánchez de Bustamante, the sociologist Fernando Ortiz, the painter Leopoldo Romanach, and the composers Sánchez de Fuente and Amadeo Roldán won international acclaim. They formed the vanguard of a contemporary movement that has produced a number of outstanding figures in arts and letters. Among the most noteworthy are the essayists Jorge Mañach, Juan J. Remos, and José M. Chacón y Calvo; and the novelist Alejo Carpentier. Among contemporary artists of Hemisphere-wide renown are Fidelio Ponce, Amelia Peláez, Wilfredo Lam, and the sculptor, Juan José Sicre.

Folk music is exceptionally rich in Cuba. Afro-Cuban rhythms in their diverse dance forms are universally renowned. The popular music and song that made Ernesto Lecuona and Gonzalo Roig world famous have many other talented interpreters in Cuba.

**Economy.** Cuba's main exports are sugar, tobacco, nickel, and fruits. The principal industries are sugar refining, cigarettes and cigars, rum, and textiles.

# DOMINICAN REPUBLIC
Population: 4.3 million

THE DOMINICAN REPUBLIC, which shares the island of Hispaniola with Haiti, figures prominently in the history of the New World as the jumping-off point for conquest and colonization of the Indies.

**Geography.** The Dominican Republic occupies the eastern two thirds of the island that Columbus called La Española (Hispaniola), in the center of the Greater Antilles. Four nearly parallel mountain ranges, covered by dense vegetation, traverse the country from east to west. The largest of these, the Central Cordillera, divides the republic into two equal parts. Duarte Peak (10,206 feet), the highest in the West Indies, is in this range. To the north is the Cordillera Septentrional and to the south the Sierra Neiba and the Sierra de Bahoruco. The Cibao, or Vega Real, located between the Central and Septentrional cordilleras, is the largest and most fertile valley, the breadbasket and livestock producing area of the country. Santo Domingo is the capital of the republic and its main city and port. Next in importance are Santiago de los Cabelleros, the commercial center of the Cibao Valley; Puerto Plata; San Pedro de Macorís; and Montecristi.

**History.** The city of Santo Domingo, founded in 1496, is the oldest European settlement in the Hemisphere. The first viceroy of the Americas, Diego Columbus, son of the Admiral, lived in the Alcázar, which has been restored as a museum.

The first colonists on the island built many sugar-cane mills and cultivated the fertile valleys, despite frequent raids by pirates. As the Conquest progressed on the mainland and people moved to the new lands, the island's population declined. In 1697 France gained control of the western third of the island (now Haiti), and the eastern part was ceded to France in 1795. Thus Santo Domingo began a long and harrowing period of uncertainty and struggles that included invasion by the troops of the Haitian general Toussaint L'Ouverture, recovery by Spain, expulsion of the Spanish governor, and the movement to incorporate the country into Gran Colombia. Then came a second Haitian occupation, this time for a period of twenty-two years. In the middle of the nineteenth century, three independence leaders, "La Trinitaria," led by Juan Pablo Duarte, appealing to the patriotism of the people, succeeded in winning the sovereignty of the Dominican nation. Independence was proclaimed on February 27, 1844. However, internal political rivalries prevented development of the country, and a new movement toward annexation re-established Spanish rule, though only briefly. Spain definitively surrendered its claim to the Dominican Republic in 1865. Following successive episodes of United States intervention, the full sovereignty of the Dominican nation was restored in 1924.

Rafael L. Trujillo dominated the political scene until his violent death in 1961. In internal conflict in 1965, which led to the involvement of United States troops and an OAS peace force, was followed by a return to constitutional democracy. Joaquín Balaguer was re-elected President in 1970.

**Culture.** Cradle of western civilization in the New World, the city of Santo Domingo preserves, in addition to the Alcázar, the first cathedral in America and the historic ruins of the first university, the first customs house, the first hospital, and other outstanding civic buildings. The cathedral contains the tomb of Christopher Columbus himself, who wished to remain there forever.

Dominican intellectuals of note have included Félix María del Monte, Federico Henríquez Carvajal, Pedro Enríquez Ureña and Salome Ureña, Gaston F. Deligne, Manuel Galván, and Manuel Peña Battle. Dominican popular music shares many of the common characteristics of an Afro-Antillean background, owing to the large population drawn from that source and the extinction of other groups of pure Indian descent. As in the other islands of the Caribbean, carvings of the precious woods native to the region predominate in Dominican crafts.

**Economy.** The Dominican Republic's principal export crops are sugar, cacao, and coffee. The major industries are sugar milling, food processing, beverages, cement, and textiles. Iron ore, bauxite, salt, gypsum, and nickel are mined.

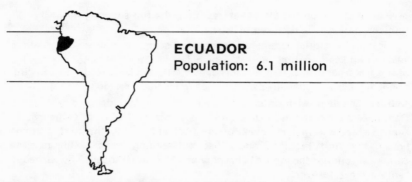

**ECUADOR**
Population: 6.1 million

WITH ITS THREE distinct regions—the coast, the sierra, and the jungle—Ecuador boasts a variety of climates, scenery, and forms of cultural expression. The country is particularly famous for its magnificent colonial art and architecture.

**Geography.** Two parallel Andes ranges cross Ecuador from north to south, linked by small spurs that create the fertile, temperate Andean valleys. Dominating the plateaus are twenty-two mountains reaching heights of from fourteen thousand to more than twenty thousand feet. Chimborazo is the highest peak in the country and Cotopaxi the highest active volcano in the world. A fertile lowland rich in tropical crops stretches between the sierra and the Pacific coast, while east of the mountains, toward the great Amazon basin, the land becomes a humid jungle, rich in petroleum.

The Galapagos Islands or Colón Archipelago, located on the equator six hundred miles off shore, belong to Ecuador. These islands, renowned for their flora and fauna and their volcanic composition, have fascinated the famous men of science who have visited them, including Charles Darwin.

Quito, the capital of Ecuador, lies in the shadow of Pichincha volcano, at 9,300 feet. It preserves an invaluable architectural and artistic heritage of the colonial centuries when it was the headquarters of a vast, rich territory extending far beyond the present boundaries of the country, the Audiencia of Quito. Guayaquil is the largest city and most important port in the country. Cuenca, with its long tradition of culture, and Riobamba and Ambato are also major centers. Otavalo, famous for its Indian fairs, is located in the north.

**History.** The territory of Ecuador was conquered by the Incas at the end of the fifteenth century. A struggle between the brothers Atahualpa and Huáscar for control of the empire facilitated its conquest by the Spaniards, led by Francisco Pizarro, who landed in 1526. At the end of 1533, Atahualpa, the last Inca emperor, was taken prisoner and beheaded in Cajamarca. In 1534, Sebastián de Belalcázar founded the city of San Francisco de Quito on the site of the capital of the old Kingdom of Quitu and the empire of Atahualpa. The new city progressed so rapidly and became so important that in 1563 it was named the capital of the Royal Audiencia of Quito.

Quito's revolutionary spirit, which repeatedly demonstrated its dissatisfaction with the colonial regime, had as its mentor and guide Eugenio de Santa Cruz y Espejo, the national hero. The political writings of Espejo lighted the path to freedom. Although he died in 1795, his influence on the patriots of Colombia and Venezuela was decisive in accelerating the independence movement launched in 1809 in Quito, that established the first supreme government junta. Although the Spaniards regained control of the colony, with the support of troops called in from other colonies, after slaughtering all the members of the revolutionary junta, the Ecuadorians did not slacken in their fight for liberation. Simón Bolívar sent Antonio José de Sucre against Guayaquil, which fell to the patriots. From that port Sucre marched on Quito, fighting on the very slopes of Pichincha the decisive battle that, on May 24, 1822, won the final independence from Spanish control.

Ecuador, Colombia, and Venezuela formed Gran Colombia in accordance with the plan of the Liberator. But the new state endured only briefly. In 1830, Ecuador initiated its political existence as a sovereign state, adopted its first constitution, and elected General Juan José Flores as the first President.

The mountain and the coast, Quito and Guayaquil, conservatives and liberals displayed their mutual antagonisms, sometimes violently, in the political evolution of the republic. The conservative Flores was opposed by the liberal figure of Vicente Rocafuerte. The authoritarian and dictatorial political doctrine of Gabriel García Moreno was followed, after twenty years of civil unrest, by that of the liberal leader Eloy Alfaro, who with Leonidas Plaza brought about profound political and social reforms that marked the beginning of a new era. Periods of fierce struggle were followed by interludes of constructive peace, such as the presidencies of Leonidas Plaza, Alfredo Baquerizo Moreno, José Luis Tamayo, Galo Plaza, and Camilo Ponce Enríquez. On five occasions, José María Velasco Ibarra has served as chief of state. He was most recently elected in 1968.

**Culture.** The most impressive evidence of Ecuador's pre-Columbian past is the citadel of Ingapirca on the Andean plateau, although a wealth of ceramic pieces and ornate gold work of the most diverse origins has also been found. The strong Indian roots of the present population have been combined with Spanish traits, but communities of pure Indian descent still exist, such as those of the Otavalos, excellent artisans; the Colorados; the Jivaros; and the Aucas. Since the very first years of the colony, the Royal Audiencia of Quito was distinguished by its masterful artistry. Its school of sculptors, led by Caspicara, has no peer in the Americas. The altarpieces of Quito and Cuenca, together with the incomparable pulpit of Guápulo, are genuine masterpieces of carving. Miguel de Santiago and Bernardo Legarda made the painting of the Quito school famous, but religious architecture most properly represents the high point of colonial art. The churces of La Compañia, San Francisco, Santo Domingo, and La Merced are magnificent examples of the Quito baroque.

Printing was introduced in the middle of the eighteenth century, and from that time on books and newspapers published the thoughts of the country's finest men of letters, of whom Gaspar de Villarroel and Eugenio Espejo formed the vanguard. At the beginning of the nineteenth century Ecuadorian poetry was represented by José Joaquin Olmedo, and in the Romantic period by Remigio Crespo-Toral, among others. But the most outstanding figure of the era was Juan Montalvo, the symbol of liberal ideas. In succeeding generations of Ecuadorian intellectuals several names stand out, including Federico González Suarez and Gonzalo Zaldumbide, and among contemporaries the novelist Jorge Icaza, Benjamin Carrión, and the poet Jorge Carrera-Andrade. Among the numerous painters in Ecuador today, Oswaldo Guayasamín has attained international renown. Inevitably, the sierra and the coast have left their own special impressions on the rich variety of Ecuadorian folk arts. The so-called Panama hats, made of toquilla straw, are handwoven in Ecuador.

**Economy.** Agriculture accounts for 37 per cent of Ecuador's GNP; industry for 16 per cent. Principal exports are bananas, coffee, cacao, petroleum, pharmaceuticals and rice.

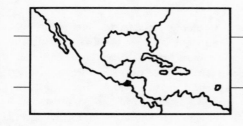

# EL SALVADOR
## Population: 3.4 million

THIS IS THE smallest and most densely populated of the Central American republics and the only one with a single coast, on the Pacific; yet it is the region's largest exporter of coffee and one of its most heavily industrialized countries. El Salvador is famous for its volcanoes and its fragrant balsam trees. Its capital was once the capital of the Federation of the United Provinces of Central America and is today the headquarters of the Organization of Central American States (ODECA).

**Geography.** El Salvador is composed of very mountainous terrain. Two cordilleras cross the country from west to east and a series of fourteen volcanoes stretches along the coast. Between these mountains and the Pacific lies the sugar-cane zone, while between the coastal cordillera and the northern sierra a region of subtropical plateaus is dotted with many fertile valleys. The prairies of the Lempa Basin are used mainly for stock raising. The eastern part of the country is hot, producing cotton and henequen. Coffee, the basis of the national economy, is grown on the fertile temperate slopes of the mountains east of the Lempa River and in the fairly high western part of El Salvador, between San Salvador and the Guatemalan border.

There are many geysers in the volcanic desert near Ahuachapán; Lake Ilopango, the largest in the republic, occupies the crater of an old volcano. Lake Guija, which empties into the Lempa River, is of interest to archaeologists because of the ancient ruins found on its islands and shores. Izalco volcano was known as the "Lighthouse of the Pacific" because of its constant activity. The capital is San Salvador, an extraordinarily progressive and industrious city. The second most important center is Santa Ana, set in a beautiful valley, followed by San Miguel and Sonsonate, both of which are becoming industrial centers. La Unión is the major port in the country; two others, La Libertad and Acajutla, with a fine bathing beach, are also important.

**History.** The Spanish conquistador Pedro de Alvarado reached El Salvador in 1524. After defeating the Indians, he founded the city of San Salvador de Cuscatlán in April of the following year. In 1542, the colony became part of the Captaincy General of Guatemala, together with what are now the Republics of Guatemala, Honduras, Nicaragua, and Costa Rica, and the Mexican State of Chiapas. The chief hero of the independence was Father José Matías Delgado, who, in November 1811, directed the first attempt at liberation. In 1821, the Captaincy General of Guatemala declared its independence from Spain. When the Mexican empire sought to annex the Central American provinces, El Salvador resisted, fighting off the Mexican forces until the fall of Emperor Agustín de Iturbide in 1823. The Constitution of El Salvador, published on June 12, 1824, was the first adopted in Central America. In 1834, the Central American Federation capital was moved to San Salvador and subsequently to Sonsonate. In 1841, the National Assembly of El Salvador formally proclaimed its separation from the Federation. Twentieth century governments have generally maintained order and peace, which has permitted significant development. Since 1948, after the political crisis that put an end to dictatorial regimes, more progressive governments have come to power. President Fidel Sánchez Hernández was elected in 1967.

**Culture.** The Salvadorian people have strong roots in the Mayan culture, of which they still conserve many traces. One of the important tribes that inhabited what is today the territory of El Salvador was the Pipil, probably related to the Aztecs of Mexico. The present population results from the mixture of Spaniards and Indians. A few of the latter, among them the Panchos of Panchimalco and the Izalcos, preserve their ancient customs and traditions.

Dances of the sun-worshipping Pipil Indians can be seen around Sonsonate and Ahuachapán, which are authentic Indian villages. The same is true of the towns of Izalco and Nahuizalco, noted for the charm and color of their costumes, and finally Panchimalco, ancient seat of the Pancho Indians, which is a source of special interest to ethnologists.

Spanish colonial architecture is almost entirely religious; it is simple, well proportioned, and graceful in design. Because of the continual earthquakes, buildings are usually low, with thick walls. The cathedral of Santa Ana is one of the finest in the country.

Francisco Morazán, the apostle of Central American union, made an initial contribution to the improvement of public education, but perhaps the decisive momentum for the development of Salvadorian culture was provided during the administration of Francisco Dueñas (1863-71). The country now has many cultural institutions and a good university, the successor to the old College of La Asunción authorized by the 1841 Constitution. Francisco Gavida and Alberto Masferrer, among others, were pioneers in the movement, which has produced a number of outstanding figures.

**Economy.** Agriculture accounts for about 30 per cent of the GNP; manufacturing, stimulated by the Central American Common Market, for about 20 per cent. Industries include food products, shoes, clothing, textiles, and cement. Coffee, cotton, and sugar are the principal exports.

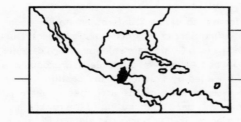

## GUATEMALA
### Population: 5.1 million

CRADLE AND SEAT of the Mayan civilization, Guatemala is a country favored by a pleasant climate, beautiful scenery, picturesque villages, and a significant complex of striking historical monuments.

**Geography.** The territory of Guatemala can be divided into two geographic zones: the lowland zones of the Pacific and Caribbean coasts and the Department of Petén, and the temperate zone of the plateaus and cordilleras that extend from northwest to southeast, covering two thirds of the country. Some of the thirty-three volcanoes in Guatemala are among the highest peaks in Central America: Tajumulco, Tacaná, Acatenango, Fuego, Santa María, and Agua. Fuego and Santa María are still active. The Department of Petén, located to the north, is a sparsely populated forested plain containing vast quantities of such fine woods as cedar, mahogany, ebony, and walnut, in addition to rubber trees. Lake Atitlán, Lake Izabal, and the Dulce River are points of great scenic beauty.

Guatemala City, the national capital, is a modern cosmopolitan metropolis and the largest city in Central America. Quezaltenango, with its colonial ambience, is the next important, while Puerto Barrios, on the Caribbean, is the chief port in the country.

**History.** The Classic period of Mayan civilization dates from around A.D. 300 to 900. It was during that period that the Mayas built their great cities, of which Tikal, in the Guatemalan Petén, is a magnificent example.

The colonial history of the country began amid the ruins of its great Indain past, when Pedro de Alvarado conquered the territory and founded the city of Santiago de los Caballeros de Goathemala, which was twice destroyed and twice changed to a new site. Of the first founding, in 1524, only a few traces remain. The second, also a victim of the fury of successive earthquakes and volcanoes, was buried in the debris of a tragic flood. But Antigua, as the last site is known today, preserves evidence of its ancient splendor and grandeur. This city was the headquarters of the Captaincy General and seat of the Audiencia for all of Central America in colonial times. After gaining independence from Spain in 1824, the region was annexed to the Mexican empire of Agustín de Iturbide, and later became a part of the Federation of United Provinces of Central America in 1823. Political disagreements destroyed the effort in 1838 and Guatemala established its own government, becoming a republic in 1847. The reformist process that contributed decisively to the formation of the Guatemalan nation began much later, in 1873, when Justo Rufino Barrios took office as President. During the period of Jorge Ubico (1931-1944), Guatemala enjoyed an era of order and peace. The Presidency of Jacobo Arbenz, a radical leftist, produced a violent military reaction in 1954 headed by Colonel Carlos Castillo Armas. Since the new Constitution of 1966, in spite of the activities of terrorist groups, democratic governments have been contributing to the progressive development of this rich nation. Carlos Arana Osorio was elected President in 1970.

**Culture.** The **Popol-Vuh,** the sacred book of the Maya-Quiché, constitutes the literary monument par excellence of the aboriginal past. Contemporary thought and literature had their beginning at the Pontifical University of San Carlos Borromeo, founded in 1681, and the Economic Society of Friends of Guatemala, constituted in 1797. The predecessor of the true national literature was Antonio José de Irisarri, and the first of its great poets was José Batres y Montúfar. Among the writers of the transition to the twentieth century, Enrique Gómez Carrillo stands out.

The country's rapid development in recent decades has transformed the face of its cities, proliferated educational and cultural facilities, and generated a strong intellectual movement. Miguel Angel Asturias, the great novelist, won the Nobel Prize for literature in 1967.

A popular tourist attraction is Chichicastenango, a living folk museum and Indian market center.

**Economy.** Coffee and cotton remain Guatemala's principal products, but the Central American Common Market has stimulated production of tires, clothing, foodstuffs, and pharmaceuticals. Nickel mining is an important new activity.

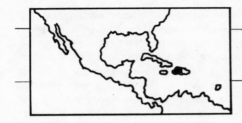

**HAITI**
Population: 5.2 million

THE TROPICAL GREEN MOUNTAINS of Haiti have borne witness to an extraordinary history. The first black republic in the world and the only French-speaking independent nation in America, she was also the first Latin American nation to gain independence.

**Geography.** Haiti occupies the western part of the island of Hispaniola, sharing it with the Dominican Republic. The capital, Port-au-Prince, lies at the point on the Gulf of Gonaïves where the country's two mountainous peninsulas converge. The second city and colonial capital, Cap-Haïtien, is on the northern coast. Coffee plantations climb the terraces of the three mountain ranges that cover two-thirds of the interior, and sugar cane plantations spread over the verdant lowlands that lie between the mountains.

**History.** In 1492, not far from Cap-Haïtien, Columbus built the Fort of La Natividad. The entire island of Hispaniola was under the Spanish until French colonizers became established there and France acquired the western third (Haiti), which they called Saint Domingue, in 1697. The many successful coffee plantations established by the French made the region one of the richest colonies in America, a prosperity that did not extend to the thousands of slaves.

On the outbreak of the French Revolution in 1789, Haiti's Negro slaves sought emancipation. When their leaders, Vincent Ogé and Jean-Baptiste Chavannes, were executed, the slaves began a revolt that sowed destruction and death throughout the land. It was then that Toussaint L'Ouverture assumed leadership. He had become a general in the French Army and Governor of Saint Domingue. To break Toussaint's control, Napoleon sent a powerful expedition under the command of his brother-in-law, General Leclerc, to establish French authority once more. After many fierce battles, Toussaint was lured into a trap, captured, and sent to France, where he died a prisoner. Two Haitian generals formerly in the French Army carried on the war: the Haitian national hero, Jean Jacques Dessalines, and Alexandre Pétion. The French were defeated, after a long struggle, in 1803.

On January 1, 1804, Dessalines proclaimed the country's independence and adopted the original Indian name of Haiti. Dessalines, appointed governor general for life, took the title of emperor. He was assassinated in 1806, and the country was divided into a northern monarchy under King Christophe and a southern republic under Pétion, a friend and admirer of

Bolívar. Christophe (Henri I) was a former slave who had fought against the British during the American Revolution and had played a decisive part in the defeat of General Leclerc. Fearing the return of the French, he built the Citadel, an impregnable fortress and one of the Hemisphere's most imposing monuments; and to lodge his large court he constructed the Palace of Sans Souci. After Christophe's suicide in 1820, the country was reunited under John Pierre Boyer, and Haiti occupied the Spanish part of the island for twenty-two years. A political and economic crisis brought on the intervention of the United States in Haiti in 1915. Control of the country returned to Haitian hands in 1934 during the administration of Stenio Vincent. François Duvalier became President in 1957 and "President-for-Life" in 1964.

**Culture.** Haiti is a country of contrasts, formed in adversity, without great natural resources, but proud of her traditions and extraordinarily sensitive to all that concerns the nation's independence. There has been no lack of first-rate intellectuals, among them Antoine Dupré, Jean Price Mars, Émile Roumer, Roussan Camille, Masillon Coicon, who brought creole speech to the literary scene, and Jacques Roumain, one of Haiti's greatest novelists.

Haitian culture has been most famous for folk art—particularly its well-known primitive painters, who have also given us beautiful examples of mural painting. French is the official language and French influence can be seen in the architecture, especially in Cap-Haïtien. Not far from that city are the architectural jewels of the Citadel and Sans Souci, now in ruins, and other evocative monuments like the palace of Pauline Bonaparte, wife of General Leclerc, and the fortresses of Magny and Picolet. African beliefs mingled with western tradition and Indian elements make up the cult of Voodoo and are reflected in many carnivalesque events.

**Economy.** Haiti is primarily an agricultural country, the chief products being coffee, sugar, sisal, cotton, and cacao. Industry is largely limited to food processing and the manufacture of textiles, soap, and cement. The chief exports are coffee, sugar, bauxite, sisal, and copper.

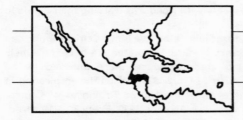

**HONDURAS**
Population: 2.7 million

THE SECOND LARGEST of the Central American republics, Honduras is a mountainous country rich in natural resources and proud of its Maya heritage.

**Geography.** The Central American cordillera crosses the country from northwest to southeast. The plains extending from the northern coast into the interior are noted for their large banana plantations. Swamps, mountains and jungles cover the eastern coast of Mosquitia. The central plateau, with broad valleys and sloping hills, accounts for 65 per cent of the national territory and 70 per cent of the population. The beautiful Lake Yojoa, located in the Jicoque Mountains, is the pride of the country. The picturesque Bay Islands belong to Honduras. The only Honduran port on the Pacific is Amapala, on Tiger Island, one of the islands in the Gulf of Fonseca.

Despite urban progress the mountain city of Tegucigalpa, the capital of Honduras and its major commercial center, retains its original style of construction and its attractive terraced streets. The second largest city is San Pedro Sula, a center for banana growing and industries derived from sugar cane, and the principal distribution center for the northern and western areas of the republic. Choluteca, located on the broad and beautiful plain of the river of the same name, is a stock-raising and coffee-producing center. La Ceiba, on the Caribbean, is the largest port in Honduras.

**History.** The country was discovered by Christopher Columbus in 1502, when he landed for the first time in Central America. The city of Comayagua was founded in 1537 as capital of the province. The Indians were subdued at the end of the 1530's, when their chief, Lempira, was treacherously killed during a peace conference. The name of Lempira, which is also given to the country's monetary unit, has become a Honduran symbol of freedom and nationalism.

In 1539 Honduras became part of the Captaincy General of Guatemala; for almost the entire period up to 1821 it was divided into two provinces: Tegucigalpa and Comayagua. In 1578, silver deposits were found in the hills around Tegucigalpa, an Indian name derived from **tegus galpa,** meaning "mountain of silver." Because of its mineral wealth and growing economic importance, Honduras was frequently attacked by French, English, and Dutch pirates. In the seventeenth century, the Mosquito Indians settled in the area of Mosquitia and asked the English for protection; with this help, they defeated the Spanish forces. British forces occupied the region up to

1859, when the English signed a treaty with Honduras waiving their rights to the Mosquitia territory.

On September 15, 1821, Honduras joined the five other Central American provinces comprising the Captaincy General of Guatemala to declare their independence from Spain. All of these provinces were annexed to the Mexican empire of Agustín de Iturbide (1822-1823). When the empire fell in 1823, Honduras joined the Federation of the United Provinces of Central America, whose first president was José Arce. In 1830, Francisco Morazán, the national hero of Honduras and champion of Central American unity, became the second president of the Federation. Morazán carried out many social and economic reforms, but despite his efforts to preserve the Federation it was dissolved, and in 1838 Honduras went its own way. The first constitutional President, Francisco Ferrer, took office in January 1841. In the first decades after independence when various attempts were made to revive the Federation, there was much institutional and political instability. In 1932 Tiburcio Carías became President and the party he led stayed in power until 1957 when Ramón Villeda Morales was elected. In 1965 the country was given a new Constitution and in that year Colonel Oswaldo López Arellano was elected President.

**Culture.** Indians and Spaniards, unmixed with other immigrant strains, are the basic components of the nation's population. As an exception, owing to alternate possession of the territory by Spain and England, many descendants of Englishmen and Africans are found on the Bay Islands and in Mosquitia. The first university in Central America was established in the colonial capital of Comayagua in 1632. The cathedral of Comayagua, dating from the seventeenth century, is a magnificent example of early colonial architecture. Eloquent proof of the Mayan tradition that still underlies the rich Honduran folk arts are the ruins of the ancient city of Copán, outstanding for the majestic grandeur of its temples and the magnificence of their rich carvings and abundant hieroglyphics.

The cultural evolution of the nation, beginning in the middle of the last century, produced men of international stature. José Cecilio del Valle, Ramón Rosa, and Alberto Membreño exerted a decisive influence on the philosophy of Central American unity, while Juan Ramón Molina and Heliodoro Valle headed a legion of outstanding intellectuals. José Antonio Velásquez is a prominent contemporary painter.

**Economy.** About 40 per cent of Honduras' GNP comes from agriculture and 14 per cent from industry, which consists mainly of light consumer goods. Bananas, coffee, and lumber are the principal exports.

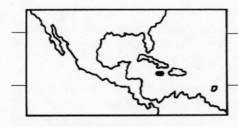

**JAMAICA**
Population: 2 million

THIS PROGRESSIVE YOUNG NATION is capitalizing on its great tourist potential to accelerate its economic and social development. Jamaica is the newest member state of the OAS.

**Geography.** The original Arawak inhabitants called the island Xaymaca, which means land of woods and streams. It is also said that when Sir Henry Morgan wished to describe the new discovery to the Queen of England, he tightly crumpled a piece of paper and threw it on the table, to demonstrate the unevenness of the terrain. The mountain massif at the eastern end consists of the Blue Mountains, whose highest peak rises 7,402 feet above sea level. But, generally speaking, the country's mountains are low and gently sloping, with a cover of tropical vegetation, and well suited to farming.

The capital and largest city of the island is Kingston, where one third of the country's total population resides and where its commercial and industrial activity is concentrated. This is also the major port. Situated at the other end of the island is Montego Bay, a tourist mecca.

**History.** After Jamaica's discovery in 1494 the Arawaks were soon subdued. The island was brought under the authority of Hispaniola in 1509, administered by Diego Columbus, the Admiral's eldest son. Juan de Esquivel was sent out to govern the new colony and founded its first capital, Sevilla la Nueva. The capital was later moved to a site near Villa de la Vega, known today as Spanish Town. The comparatively greater importance of other discoveries caused a progressive decline in the standing of this colony and it eventually fell into English hands despite resistance from Jamaican creoles, who continued to wage guerrilla warfare for many years. The English founded Port Royal in 1655 and built the stronghold of Fort Charles. The island became a center for pirate operations against the Spanish empire. Morgan personified that period of Jamaican history. Shortly after his death, in 1688, a terrible earthquake destroyed Port Royal and led to the establishment of Kingston on the other side of the bay. Emancipation in 1838, followed by an economic recession, set the stage for an 1865 rebellion led by Paul Bogle, who was executed together with the Assemblyman George William Gordon and over three hundred Negroes. Dr. Robert Love further strengthened the political voice of Black Jamaicans at the turn of the century. In 1938 Alexander Bustamante founded the Labour Party and Norman Washington Manley the National People's Party. In 1944, the island adopted a new Constitution. In 1958, Jamaica joined the Federation of the West Indies, from which it separated in 1961. Finally, it proclaimed its independence on August 6, 1962. Sir Alexander Bustamante served as the first Prime Minister and head of the Government of Jamaica. Hugh Shearer was elected Prime Minister in 1967.

**Culture.** Jamaica's history has been accompanied, step by step, by the formation of a national identity. The determining factor in the social process was necessarily the population of African descent, which has constituted a majority on the island since the eighteenth century. Pioneers of Jamaican literature were Tom Redcam, Herbert George DeLisser, and Claude McKay. More recent figures are Vic Reid, Roger Mais, and John Hearne. The National Dance Theater Company has won international acclaim.

**Economy.** Jamaica is the world's largest producer of bauxite. Sugar is the principal employer on the island, but manufacturing now contributes more to GNP than agriculture. Chief exports are bauxite, alumina, sugar, rum, molasses, and bananas. Tourism is also an important source of income.

# MEXICO
## Population: 50.7 million

THE MOST POPULOUS Spanish-speaking country in the world, Mexico is noted for its scenic beauty and its rapid economic growth, as well as a rich cultural heritage.

**Geography.** The vast agricultural region of Mexico runs from north to south between the two great mountain chains of the Sierra Madre, the Western and the Eastern ranges. The tropical lands along the Gulf coast differ in topography, climate, and economy from the central plateau, the highlands of Chiapas, and the peninsulas of Yucatán and Baja California. This panoramic diversity is one of the country's major tourist attractions. Veracruz and Tampico on the Gulf of Mexico and Manzanillo and Acapulco on the Pacific are the largest bays, and the beaches at Acapulco are famous throughout the world.

The peaks of Orizaba and Popocatépetl, the latter not far from Mexico City, are the highest in the Sierra. More than fifty national parks and reservations safeguard an immense wealth of forest resources, and progressive utilization of water resources is making the vast desert lands in the North and in Baja California productive. Equally dynamic is the forward-looking effort being made to bring much of jungle-covered Yucatán into the national economy.

Mexico City, located on the very site of the Aztec city of Tenochtitlán, is the federal capital of the United Mexican States and the focus of the nation's economic and cultural life. The city is the urban center of an extensive metropolitan area almost as populous as New York. In addition to its magnificent capital, the country boasts such other major cities as Guadalajara, center of a rich mining and agricultural region; Monterrey, a highly industrialized city; Puebla, "city of the angels," with its 60 churches; and Veracruz, a highly important port; as well as Mérida, Oaxaca, Querétaro, and many others that, despite their smaller size, attract visitors because of the magnificence of their churches, the charm and color of their plazas and markets, and the beauty of their settings.

**History.** The pre-Columbian peoples of Mexico, especially the Mayas, Nahuas, Olmecs, Zapotecs, and Mixtecs, left evidence of a creative architectural and artistic splendor. The outstanding achievements of the Mayas include invention of a 365-day calendar year and the construction of such magnificent temples as those at Chichén-Itzá in Yucatán. The Aztecs, for their part, also left abundant proof of their political organization and urban development. The Aztec calendar stone displayed in the National Museum of Anthropology in Chapultepec Park is the admiration of all who see it today. Aztec domination of the broad central plateau was at its height when the Spanish conquest began in 1519 with Hernando Cortez' expedition from Cuba. Exploiting internal opposition to the Aztec overlords, in two years Cortez was able to vanquish the armies of Moctezuma and to destroy his empire. The emperor's nephew, Cuauhtémoc, was the last of the Aztec rulers. Three hundred years of Spanish domination followed. In 1535, Mexico City became the seat of the Viceroyalty of New Spain, which was to rival the Viceroyalty of Peru in prosperity and riches. Architecture was the dominant artistic expression during the colonial period, and innumerable churches were founded by the propagators of the new faith in each of the cities established by the Spaniards. The imported culture made use of the Indian heritage to create combinations of artistic forms such as the Mexican baroque. Mexico can be proud of the development of ideas, letters, and arts during the colonial period. In 1539 the first book of the Americas was printed there, and in 1551 the National University was founded.

When Napoleon Bonaparte invaded Spain in 1808, patriots in Latin America seized the opportunity to act. Father Miguel Hidalgo y Costilla, raising as his standard the image of the Virgin of Guadalupe, gave the cry of independence—the **grito de Dolores.** He and Father José María Morelos were the forerunners of a liberation movement that was to revolutionize the entire country, culminating in the final downfall of the Spanish forces and Agustín de Iturbide's triumphant entry into Mexico City on September 27, 1821.

A brief imperial period began in the country, extending its influence southward into Central America. It was followed by reestablishment of the Republic with fewer civil liberties and less authentic representation of the Mexican people. Those goals were not achieved until the appearance of Benito Juárez, who was elected President in 1858. During the civil war that ensued French troops intervened and crowned the Archduke Maximilian of Austria Emperor of Mexico in 1864. Juárez, continuing his struggle from exile, succeeded in regaining control, and in 1867 the emperor was executed. In 1877, one of Juárez' generals, Porfirio Díaz, became President and ruled the country through a type of enlightened dictatorship until his overthrow by the Revolution, which began in 1910. Despite the criticism of his administration, the extended period of peace made a significant contribution to the maturity of the new Mexican nation. Francisco I. Madero was the idealistic and humanitarian exponent of the Revolutionary period, which included such other popular leaders as Venustiano Carranza and Emiliano Zapata. In 1934, General Lázaro Cárdenas was elected President, launching the contemporary period under the guidance of the Mexican Revolutionary Party.

An orderly succession of presidents, ineligible for more than one six-year term, has operated in favor of the development and progress of the Mexican nation within the framework of a liberal constitution. Luis

Echeverría Alvarez was elected President in 1970.

**Culture.** Mexican literature in the colonial era was represented by poets of the stature of Sor Juana Inés de la Cruz and writers like Juan Ruiz de Alarcón and José Joaquín Fernández de Lizardi, author of the first American novel, "El Periquillo Sarniento." In the late nineteenth and early twentieth centuries, Mexico boasted a group of first-class writers and poets, including Justo Sierra, Manuel Gutiérrez Nájera, Amado Nervo, Martín Luis Guzmán, Alfonso Reyes and José Vasconcelos. The contemporary movement is led by Jaime Torres Bodet and José Gorostiza. Mexican painting made an invaluable contribution to contemporary art through its universally famed murals, the work of the great masters Diego Rivera, José Clemente Orozco, David Alfaro Siqueiros, and Rufino Tamayo.

Composers such as Manuel M. Ponce, Silvestre Revueltas, and Carlos Chávez initiated the search for musical identity.

The soul of Mexico's people is expressed in its extraordinarily rich music, dance, and crafts, in which the Indian heritage is conjoined with many Spanish artistic and folk influences. From Aztec and colonial days to the present, the various regions have had their traditional products, and the beautifully decorated and glazed ceramic ware and the exquisite silver jewelry are known all over the world. Other items for which the country is famous are textiles, especially the colorful serapes; tooled leather, glassware, carved and painted wooden masks, lacquered bowls and trays; retables, or religious painted sculptural panels, and basketry.

**Economy.** Industry now accounts for 26 per cent of Mexico's GNP; agriculture for 17 per cent. Motor vehicles, machinery, petrochemicals, steel and cement are the principal products. Exports consist mainly of cotton, sugar, coffee, shrimp, petroleum, and minerals. Tourism is also an important source of revenue. Mexico is the world's largest producer of silver and a major producer of sulphur, lead, and zinc.

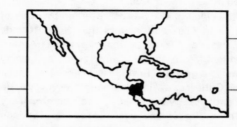

**NICARAGUA**
Population: 2 million

LARGEST OF THE CENTRAL American republics, Nicaragua is the proud homeland of one of the most famous poets in the Hemisphere, Rubén Darío.

**Geography.** The Central American cordillera divides the territory of Nicaragua into two regions. The country's most important industrial and agricultural zone is located along the Pacific lowlands, which are dominated by Lake Nicaragua, one of the largest fresh water lakes in the world, and Lake Managua. In the northwest, a chain of more than twenty volcanoes, some still partially active, rises from the level plains where coffee, sesame seed, cacao, sugar, cotton, and tobacco are grown. The eastern coast is low, swampy, and covered mainly by heavy tropical forest. In the north there is a triangular area of great ranges sloping gradually to the east, where the climate is temperate. Coffee flourishes in this zone of plantations and stock ranches.

The capital and largest city is Managua, located beside the lake that bears its name. Next in importance are Léon, whose magnificent church contains the tomb of Rubén Darío; and Granada, on the shores of Lake Nicaragua. Corinto is the country's major port on the Pacific; Bluefields is the largest on the Caribbean. In the north there is another important city, Matagalpa.

**History.** Columbus laid claim in 1502 to the territory governed by the Indian chief Nicarao, from whom the name Nicaragua is derived. Seventeen years later, Gil González Dávila explored the interior, but it was not until the cities of Granada and León were founded in 1524 that settlement of the country began. In 1610 León was moved to its present location to serve as capital of the Spanish province under the Captaincy General of Guatemala, and was the capital of the republic up to 1855. Nicaragua formed part of the Federation of the United Provinces of Central America that followed independence of the region, from its establishment in 1821 up to its dissolution as a result of internal rivalries in 1838. At that time, Nicaragua adopted its Constitution as a sovereign country. Miguel Larreynaga, a jurist and writer, was the hero of Nicaragua's independence, which was followed by years of civil struggle between political parties fighting to gain control; this served to weaken national unity and to encourage unfortunate episodes of foreign occupation. William Walker, a U.S. adventurer, succeeded in seizing power and declared himself president in 1856, although a unanimous nationalistic reaction expelled him shortly afterwards and he was ultimately executed in Honduras in 1860. Thirty years of conservative government reestablished the peace and order necessary to allow the nation to make substantial progress. Liberal leaders took over for another seventeen years, up to the political crisis that led to the United States' intervention from 1912 to 1925. A new insurrection brought a return of the United States Marines from 1926 to 1933. Later, General Anastasio Somoza became the country's leading figure, which he remained until he was assasinated in 1956. He was succeeded by his son, Luis A. Somoza. Another son, Anastasio Somoza-Debayle, was elected President in 1967.

**Culture.** Many archaeological discoveries attest to the degree of development reached by the Indian cultures within the present territory of Nicaragua. There are numerous examples of colonial architecture preserved in the cities of León and Granada. León, the country's intellectual center in the eighteenth century, was the cradle of the literary movement whose finest expression was the work of Rubén Darío. This great poet and writer was born in the small town of Metapa, now Ciudad Darío, in 1867, and returned from a long pilgrimage in Europe to die in his native Nicaragua in 1916. Santiago Argüello is, after Darío, the most distinguished representative of modernism in Nicaragua, a country of extraordinary intellectual activity and in particular of excellent poets, including, among others, Ernesto Mejía Sánchez and Ernesto Cardenal.

The School of Fine Arts in Managua began the painting tradition that is continued today by many fine artists.

Since there is little pure Indian blood in most of the population and the small African influx is confined to the Caribbean coast, Nicaraguan culture is predominantly drawn from Spanish sources. However, **mestizaje** is apparent in works written in the Nahuatl-Spanish dialect still used in Nicaragua.

**Economy.** About 30 per cent of GNP comes from agriculture and about 15 per cent from industry. Chief industries are chemicals, insecticides, food processing, and textiles. Exports include coffee, cotton, bananas, meat, and gold.

**PANAMA**
Population: 1.5 million

STRATEGICALLY LOCATED Panama is the link between the Atlantic and Pacific Oceans, the land bridge connecting North and South America, and a center for international air traffic.

**Geography.** Two mountain chains form the backbone of the isthmus, enclosing a series of fertile valleys and plains. Dense jungles cover the eastern portion and much of the rest of the coutry. The Canal Zone is a narrow strip of land leased to the United States to maintain, operate, and protect the Panama Canal. More than a thousand islands lie offshore. The most interesting are those in the San Blas Archipelago in the Caribbean. Taboga Island, in the Bay of Panama, is a popular resort, while the Pearl Islands are famous for their fishing grounds.

In Darien, an area of impenetrable jungle and great swamps, bordering Colombia, is the last unfinished section of the Pan American Highway, now in process of completion.

Modern, cosmopolitan Panama City is the capital of the country. Adjoining the Canal Zone on the Pacific, it is the center of national, cultural and economic life. Colón, the second largest center and a free port, rivals the capital in its strategic position, also at the entrance to the Canal, but on the Atlantic coast. David, the third largest city, is the capital and commercial center of the richest farming region, Chiriquí Province.

**History.** In 1502 Christopher Columbus explored the Caribbean coast and claimed it in the name of the Spanish Crown. Vasco Núñez de Balboa, in 1513, made his way across the isthmus and discovered the Pacific Ocean. The provincial governor, Pedro Arias Dávila (known as Pedrarias), moved the government seat to the Pacific side and founded Panama City in 1518; Nombre de Dios and Portobelo were built on the Atlantic side of the isthmus. Because of its commercial importance, Panama was often attacked by pirates. Portobelo, a fortress which is currently being restored, was the terminal for fleets of Spanish galleons and Spain's major customs post in the Americas for more than a century. Its stores of gold and silver from Peru were the target of many attacks. Henry Morgan destroyed Panama City in 1671, and the city was rebuilt nearby at its present location.

In 1739 Panama was included within the jurisdiction of the Viceroyalty of New Granada. In 1819 Venezuela and Colombia, having freed themselves from colonial rule, formed the Republic of Gran Colombia, and in 1821 Panama joined the federation. Simón Bolívar convoked the first Pan American Congress in Panama in 1826. Up to 1903, Panama was part of Colombia, with the exception of brief intervals when the people, emboldened by secessionist movements, demanded their freedom. The most successful separatist movement was that of 1840, captained by the national hero, Tomás Herrera, during which Panama was able to retain its independence for thirteen months. It finally won its freedom on November 3, 1903. Shortly afterwards, the country signed a treaty with the United States for construction of the Canal, a masterpiece of engineering, which was opened to international trade and transportation in 1914. Since 1960, the Panamanian flag has flown over the Canal Zone as a symbol of the nation's sovereignty over that strip of land leased to the United States. Since 1952, when José A. Remón was elected President, the successive governments have managed to make positive social and economic gains, in spite of various political crises. Demetrio B. Lakas assumed leadership of the Provisional Government Junta in 1969.

**Culture.** The Indians found by the Spaniards on the Isthmus had a comparatively advanced culture. Fine gold and ceramic objects have been unearthed in the vicinity of Chiriquí, Veraguas, and Coclé. Most of the Indian groups intermarried with the Spaniards, and the country, has received a steady influx of various other immigrant groups in addition to a large wave of African population. However, isolated tribes such as the Cuna Indians on the San Blas Islands survive unspoiled. The ruins of Old Panama City, on the outskirts of the present capital, and the museum city of Portobelo are the best examples of past colonial splendor. Prominent Panamanian intellectuals have included the essayist Justo Arosemena and poets like Gil Colunje, Demetrio Korsi, Darío Herrera and Ricardo Mir. Among other distinguished contemporary writers are Belisario Porras, Samuel Lewis, Ricardo Alfaro and A. Menendez Pereira.

The African influence is strong in Panamanian folk culture, particularly in popular music and dance. During the crowded carnivals, the appearance of the women dressed in typical **pollera** costumes preserves a delightful creole tradition.

**Economy.** Agriculture contributes about 22 per cent of Panama's GNP; manufacturing about 16 per cent. Chief industries are food processing, cement, soft drinks, and alcoholic beverages. Bananas, petroleum products, shrimp, cocoa, beef, and coffee are major exports.

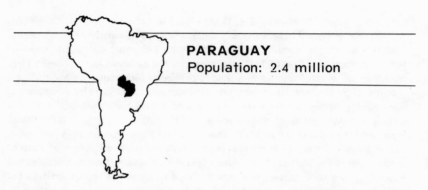

**PARAGUAY**
Population: 2.4 million

INLAND BUT NOT LANDLOCKED, Paraguay is a nation with rich forest and mineral resources, fertile soil, and an extremely colorful history.

**Geography.** Paraguay's two main waterways, the Paraná and Paraguay rivers, provide it with a direct outlet to the sea. The territory is divided in half by the Paraguay River; east of the river are tropical forests, lowland plateaus, and prairies. In the woodland clearings, land is extremely fertile, producing cotton, tobacco, sugar cane, yerba maté (also called Paraguayan tea), and a great variety of fruits. Most of the population and much of the commercial activity are concentrated in this zone of great farming and ranching wealth. To the west, the sparsely populated Chaco Boreal consists of savannas, rivers, and dense scrub forests.

In addition to the Paraguay and Paraná, the country has a third important river, the Pilcomayo, which rises in Bolivia and runs through the Chaco, forming the national boundary line on the southwest. Remarkable for their spectacular beauty are the falls of Guairá, Acaray, and Monday.

Asunción is the national capital and the center of economic and cultural activities. Its many factories are located along the banks of the Paraguay River, which forms a bay at the site of the original settlement. Other main cities are Villarrica, set in the midst of hills and orange trees; Concepción, a colonial city in the northern part of the country; Encarnación, port of embarkation for fruits, cotton, and tobacco; and Puerto Stroessner, on the Paraná, which is connected to the city of Foz do Iguaçu (Brazil) by a monumental bridge.

**History.** When Alejo García, exploring in the name of Portugal, made his journey from Brazil to Bolivia about 1520, he found that many Indians inhabited the country now known as Paraguay; the most important of the tribes was the Guaraní. Asunción was founded in 1537 and served as the nucleus of Spanish settlement in the area until Buenos Aires was founded in 1580.

Paraguay was an independent colony governed by the first creole to hold high rank in Latin America, Hernando Arias de Saavedra (Hernandarias).

It was he who pleaded successfully with the Spanish rulers to send monks to teach the Indians. This was the origin of the famous Jesuit missions, which organized a true communal society, self-sufficient and properous, whose ruins can still be seen in the border areas of Brazil, Paraguay, and Argentina. The expulsion of the Jesuit order from all Spanish territories by King Charles III in 1767 put an end to this social experiment, which had already been badly weakened by the frequent raids of Brazilian **bandeirantes** (frontiersmen).

The colonies of Paraguay and Argentina were governed by the Viceroyalty of Peru from 1617 to 1776, when the Viceroyalty of the River Plate was established to include these colonies within its jurisdiction. Paraguay became independent of Spain on May 14, 1811, when the governor resigned and a ruling council took his place. In 1814 the congress proclaimed as head of the government José Gaspar Rodríguez de Francia, known as "El Supremo." Francia ruled with an iron hand, isolating the country from the outside world. Carlos Antonio López became President in 1841 and remained in office until his death in 1862. He built roads and railroads, introduced many reforms, and promoted public education. He was succeeded by his son, Francisco Solano López, known as "El Mariscal." Under his leadership, Paraguay engaged in the devastating War of the Triple Alliance, in which Argentina, Brazil, and Uruguay allied themselves against Paraguay in a five-year struggle. The war ended with the death of López in 1870, leaving the country in ruins.

The Chaco War between Bolivia and Paraguay lasted from 1932 to 1935, when an armistice was arranged; the peace treaty was signed in 1938. This was a costly war for both countries in terms of lives and money. It was fought over conflicting claims to much of the undeveloped Gran Chaco. To resolve the controversy, Paraguay was awarded approximately two thirds of the disputed area, while Bolivia received an outlet on the Paraguay River.

José Félix Estigarribia, commander-in-chief of the Paraguayan forces in the Chaco War, was elected President in 1939 and a new Constitution adopted in 1940. The period of institutional instability and intense struggle that the country suffered until the end of World War II ended when Alfredo Stroessner became President in 1954. Stroessner was re-elected to a fourth term in 1968.

**Culture.** The Paraguayan people, formed basically from the union of Spaniards and Guaraní, still use both languages. The long period of isolation undergone by the emergent Paraguayan nation helped to affirm its native values. History and legend are contained in the works of Blas Garay, Juan E. O'Leary, and the well-known jurist Cecilio Báez, among other eminent Paraguayans of the past century. Eugenio Garay, J. Natalicio González, and Eloy Fariña Núñez continue this literary tradition, which is expressed in the Guaraní language through such outstanding poets as Manuel Ortiz Guerrero and writers like Narciso Colman and Moisés S. Bertoni. **Historia de las**

**Letras Paraguayas** (History of Paraguayan Literature), by the late Carlos R. Centurión, is an important testimony to the cultural tradition of Paraguay.

The artistic and artisan tradition of the old missions also survives in Paraguay. The delicate **ñandutí** lace, fashioned in circular design like a cobweb, which is the origin of the name in Guaraní, is justly world famous. No less attractive is the folk music of Paraguay, particularly the **guaranías** that made their appearance during the Chaco War (1932-1935).

**Economy.** About one third of Paraguay's GNP comes from agriculture and one sixth from industry. Meat packing, sugar refining, furniture, and textiles are the principal industries. Exports include meat, lumber, quebracho extract, coffee, cotton, tobacco, vegetable and essential oils.

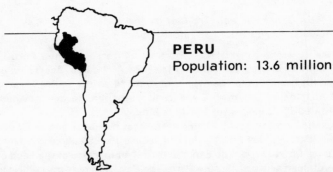

# PERU
## Population: 13.6 million

STRATEGICALLY SITUATED on the Pacific Coast of South America and generously endowed with natural resources, Peru occupied a preeminent position among Spain's viceroyalties in colonial times. Today, while cherishing its colonial heritage, Peru has increasingly become an industrial nation.

**Geography.** The three most important geographic subdivisions are the coast, the sierra, and the **montaña** (wooded foothills). The **selva,** forested lowlands in the east, might be considered as a fourth division. Three chains of Andean mountains traverse the country from north to south, dividing it into zones of contrasting climates, topography, and vegetation. The Pacific coastal desert is crossed by sixty rivers, which irrigate scores of small valleys. It seldom rains on the coast because of the effect of the cold Humboldt current from the Antarctic. The central coastal zone includes a number of islands that are the major center for production of guano, a high-quality fertilizer.

The sierra contains high peaks (Huascarán, the tallest, soars to 22,200 feet), ravines, table lands, and fertile valleys, as well as the country's major mineral deposits. Peru is the second largest producer of vanadium in the world, producing as well sizable volumes of copper, zinc, lead, gold, silver, molybdenum, iron, and petroleum. Lake Titicaca, which Peru shares with Bolivia, is the largest navigable lake in the world (12,500 feet above sea level), covering an area of 3,200 square miles on the Andean plateau and reaching a depth of up to seven hundred feet.

The **selva** extends from the foot of the Andean cordillera to the borders of Ecuador, Brazil, and Bolivia. Lima, the "City of Kings," is the capital of the republic and its most important industrial, cultural, and commercial center. Callao, the major industrial port, has one of the finest and most modern harbor installations in South America; Cuzco, the ancient and venerable capital of the Inca empire, possesses a unique complex of colonial buildings, in addition to pre-Columbian temples, fortresses, and palaces. Nearby are the ruins of Machu Picchu, the tourist mecca of Peru. Cerro de Pasco is the center of one of the oldest mining communities in South America. Arequipa, at the foot of the majestic El Misti volcano, is the second largest city in the country and the economic axis of the south's rich agricultural zone. Pisco, Chimbote, and Trujillo, on the Pacific, Iquitos, on the Amazon, and Ayacucho and Talara are other important cities.

**History.** At the time the conquistador Francisco Pizarro reached Peru in 1532, a civil war was in progress between the Inca Atahualpa, sovereign of the north, and his brother, the Inca Huáscar, who ruled the south. Pizarro overcame Atahualpa at Cajamarca and condemned him to death, which greatly facilitated his conquest of the Inca empire.

In the colonial era, Peru was the richest, most powerful and most important of the viceroyalties and the last to secure its independence from Spain. In 1820 the liberator José de San Martín left Valparaíso at the head of an Argentine-Chilean army to liberate Peru. The Peruvian patriots rallied to his ranks, and on July 28, 1821, Peru declared itself a sovereign and independent nation. The decisive engagement was fought by troops commanded by General Antonio José de Sucre, who defeated the Spaniards at the Battle of Ayacucho on December 9, 1824.

In 1866 Spain made a final effort to recover its rich colony, but was defeated at the Battle of Callao. The possession of territories bordering on Chile and Bolivia that were exceptionally rich in nitrates was the cause of a war with those countries from 1879 to 1883, which cost Peru the provinces of Tarpacá and Arica. With the administration of President Nicolás de Piérola, Peru initiated a period of reconstruction beset by domestic difficulties and political rivalries.

Beginning in 1924, the Popular American Revolutionary Party (APRA), led by Víctor Raúl Haya de la Torre, played an important role in public life, directly or indirectly shaping its political future. A junta headed by General Juan Velasco Alvarado assumed control of the government in 1968.

**Culture.** Archaeological discoveries from the Chavín, Mochica, Paracas, Nazca, and Inca cultures, among others, are dazzling in their perfection and beauty. The influence of the Cuzco school of sculpture and painting spread through the entire continent during the height of Spanish rule. The University of San Marcos in Lima was founded in 1551, and later in that century the Inca Garcilaso de la Vega wrote his famous **Royal Commentaries.** The foremost leaders in the colony's intellectual awakening were Dr. José Hipólito Unanue, physician and statesman; Isidoro de Celis, José Banquijano, and Toribio Rodrízuez de Mendoza, called the "Beacon of Peru." The arrival of the first printing press in 1583 stimulated literary efforts. The second half of the nineteenth century produced two of Peru's greatest writers, Ricardo Palma and Manuel González Prada. Palma wrote the famous **Tradiciones Peruanas.** After the turn of the century the following writers won recognition: Francisco García Calderón, José Santos Chocano, César Vallejo, and the symbolist poet Jose M. Eguren. Among this century's writers who should be mentioned are Luis Alberto Sánchez, José Carlos Mariátegui, the historian Jorge Basadre, the novelist Ciro Alegría, and the archaeologist Julio Tello.

Peruvian folk arts, particularly rich in painting and sculpture, exhibit a varied repertory of typical forms and designs in both the sierra and the coast. Exquisite fabrics continue today the tradition of excellent textiles from Paracas. The musical repertory is no less varied and interesting.

**Economy.** Peru rivals Japan as the world's leading fishing nation. About 25 per cent of Peru's GNP comes from agriculture and fishing; 19 per cent from manufacturing; and 16 per cent from mining. Principal exports are fish-meal, copper, iron, silver, sugar, and cotton.

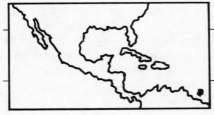

# TRINIDAD AND TOBAGO
Population: 1.1 million

TRINIDAD AND NEIGHBORING TOBAGO, together with a group of smaller islands, form the nation known today as Trinidad and Tobago, one of the new member states of the OAS. The distinguishing feature of these islands is their mixed population, which lives together in democratic harmony. Trinidad has a bustling, cosmopolitan air. Tobago, quiet and romantic, is noted for its white coral beaches and its abundant tropical vegetation.

**Geography.** Trinidad, the southernmost island in the Caribbean, is located fifteen miles off the northeast coast of Venezuela. The island is about forty-eight miles long and thirty-five wide. The low mountains that cross the island are a prolongation of a Venezuelan cordillera. Two outstanding physical features of Trinidad are Maracas Falls, in the north, and the great Pitch Lake in the south.

The island of Tobago, covering an area of 116 square miles, is situated twenty miles northeast of Trinidad. It is volcanic in origin and formed by a single mountain mass rising in gentle slopes from the coral beaches. A number of caves, bays, and tranquil beaches line the coast. The smaller islands belonging to the national territory include Little Tobago, an enchanting bird sanctuary, and the only place outside of New Guinea where the Bird of Paradise can be seen in the wild.

The country's capital, Port of Spain, is an attractive city surrounded by green hills. San Fernando and Arima are the next largest cities. Scarborough is the main city of Tobago. A mile off Tobago's northwest coast is Bucco Reef, a snorkler's paradise.

**History.** When Columbus glimpsed the three peaks of the island on the horizon in 1498, he called it Trinidad, in honor of the Holy Trinity. At that time, the island was inhabited by Caribs, a very warlike Indian tribe, and by more peaceful Arawaks. In the seventeenth century, the islands were attacked by Dutch and French pirates. During the French Revolution, many families emigrated from Haiti and other Caribbean settlements to Trinidad. Later, in 1797, during the Napoleonic Wars, a British expedition occupied the island, which was ceded to Great Britain in 1802. Tobago, in turn, was ceded by Spain to England, later to the Netherlands, and still later to France. Finally, France ceded it to England in 1814. Tobago formed part of the colony of the

Windward Islands until 1899, when it became an administrative unit of the Trinidad group.

The two islands were governed as a Crown Colony with some degree of autonomy until January 1958, when, with Jamaica, Barbados, and the Windward and Leeward Islands, they established the Federation of the West Indies. The Federation was dissolved in 1962. Trinidad and Tobago became an independent nation within the British Commonwealth on August 31, 1962.

The Crown is represented by the Governor General. The head of government is the Prime Minister, who is responsible to Parliament. Dr. Eric Williams was elected Prime Minister in 1966.

**Culture.** Trinidad has one of the most cosmopolitan populations in the world. Africans, British, Chinese, Spaniards, French, East Indians, Lebanese, Portuguese, and Syrians live here in harmony. Mosques, Hindu temples, and Victorian mansions give the urban architecture a picturesque and characteristic appeal. The complete accord in which these diverse peoples live is most apparent during Carnival, when throngs of merrymakers converge on Port of Spain.

Afro-Antillean music acquires a special accent in Trinidad and Tobago, where limbo dancing and steel bands were born. Two of the young nation's most known novelists are V. S. Naipaul and Samuel Selvon.

**Economy.** Petroleum and petroleum products are the mainstay of Trinidad and Tobago's economy. Other significant exports are sugar, cacao, and chemical fertilizers. Tourism is becoming an important source of income.

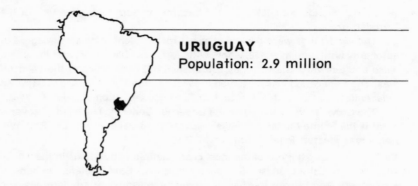

## URUGUAY
Population: 2.9 million

THE REPUBLIC OF URUGUAY is one of South America's smallest nations. Its flat expanse of grasslands provides the grazing that has made it one of the world's largest producers of wool, and it has many beautiful beaches heighten its attraction for tourists. Uruguay is noted for its commitment to democratic government and its advanced social legislation.

**Geography.** It is located on the eastern coast of South America, between the broad estuary of the River Plate and the southern border of Brazil. Except for the hilly area in the north, its topography is generally level and its natural waterways evenly distributed.

Almost half the country's population lives in the capital city of Montevideo. The original core of the city beside the port extends in an almost continuous series of crowded beaches and bathing resorts along the estuary of the River Plate and toward the Atlantic and the region's greatest tourist attraction, Punta del Este, whose name is synonymous with landmark inter-American meetings. Other important cities are Salto, center of citrus production and wine-making; Paisandú, in the north, a bustling industrial and commercial community; Mercedes, on the banks of the Negro River; Fray Bentos, a Uruguay River port that exports much of the country's meat output; and Colonia, one of the oldest of its cities.

**History.** The famous Spanish navigator, Juan Díaz de Solís, discovered the great estuary later known as the River Plate, landing in 1516 about a hundred miles from what is today Montevideo. In 1680, the Portuguese founded Nova Colonia do Sacramento (now Colonia), as an outpost against Spanish penetration from the other side of the River Plate, that is, Buenos Aires. The Spaniards founded Montevideo in 1726 as a bastion against the advances of the enormous Portuguese colony of Brazil. The Banda Oriental, as the eastern shore of the Uruguay River was called, became a battlefield in the long struggle against the Portuguese to win and hold the territory. Finally, the Portuguese were expelled from Colonia by the Spaniards, and in 1777 the Banda Oriental became part of the new Spanish Viceroyalty of the River Plate. In 1806, the English captured Buenos Aires and Montevideo but were driven out by the settlers.

The revolutionary movement launched in Buenos Aires in 1810 spread to the Banda Oriental, where patriots led by José Gervasio Artigas fought for independence from Spain and against the Portuguese invasion forces for a full decade. Artigas was unable to defeat the Portuguese and crossed the Uruguay River with his followers, never again to return to his own country. The Eastern Shore was annexed by the Portuguese colony of Brazil in 1821 as the Cisplatine Province. Artigas is recognized as the hero of Uruguayan independence but his goal of freedom was actually achieved by his countryman and follower, Juan Antonio Lavalleja, who, in 1825, led a band of patriots known as the "Thirty-three Immortals" across the River Plate to free the country. Independence was declared in 1825, and the three-year war to reconquer the territory located between Argentina and Brazil ended in 1828 when the three nations signed a peace treaty.

Internal political struggles and Uruguay's participation, with Argentina and Brazil, in the War of Triple Alliance against Paraguay prevented rapid progress until 1903, when José Batlle y Ordóñez, the great statesman and reformer, was elected President. His goal of adopting a system of government similar to that of Switzerland was fulfilled after his death when, in 1951, the office of President was abolished by plebiscite and the executive function was assigned to the National Government Council, composed of nine members directly elected by the people. However, on November 27, 1966, the Uruguayans voted in another plebiscite to restore the earlier system of executive power vested in a single chief of state. Jorge Pacheco Areco, vice president under Oscar D. Gestido, succeeded to the presidency upon the latter's death in 1967.

Uruguay was the first country in South America to grant suffrage to women, to legalize divorce, and to grant legal status to illegitimate children, including the right to inherit. It was one of the first to put into practice the eight-hour day for workers and introduce a comprehensive social security system.

**Culture.** Contemporary Uruguayan culture reflects the predominantly European composition of its population. The struggle for independence and the moral integrity and bravado of the Gaucho are the favorite topics of nineteenth century Uruguayan literature. Bartolomé Hidalgo is the greatest of the Gaucho poets. Another subject of interest was the Charrua Indians, chosen by Juan Zorrilla de San Martín, one of the great poets in the Hemisphere, as the heroes of his epic poetic legend **Tabaré**. Uruguay is also proud to number among its sons and daughters a philosopher known throughout the Hemisphere, José Enrique Rodó, and poets of the international stature of Delmira Agustini and Juana de Ibarbourou. The number and caliber of writers and artists produced by a country of barely three million inhabitants within its brief history is remarkable. Among the artists, special mention should be made of Joaquín Torres-García, one of the most outstanding pioneers of the contemporary abstract movement.

Uruguayan folk life shares many regional characteristics, although it contributes its own native accent in both music and crafts.

**Economy.** Industry—including meat packing, textiles, construction and building materials, beverages, and chemicals—now accounts for about 25 per cent of Uruguay's GNP, while agriculture has dropped to 15 per cent. Wool, meat, and hides remain the principal exports.

# VENEZUELA
## Population: 10.8 million

VENEZUELA IS EXCEPTIONALLY rich in natural resources, and is endowed with abundant deposits of gold, diamonds, iron, bauxite, and copper, but above all, petroleum. The country ranks first in oil exports and stands third in oil production in the world, and has the great historical honor of being the birthplace of the Liberator, Simón Bolívar.

**Geography.** Four distinct areas make up the territory of Venezuela: the highlands, to the west and along the Caribbean coast, in whose fertile valleys several of the major cities are found; the Maracaibo lowlands around freshwater Lake Maracaibo, under whose waters are some of the world's most extensive oil deposits; the **llanos,** great treeless plains of the Orinoco River basin; and the Guayana highlands, south of the Orinoco, a huge stretch of partially forested tableland extending to the Brazilian border. Bolívar Peak dominates the lofty Sierra Nevada de Mérida in the west. The Orinoco River and its tributaries, second largest river system in South America, drain about four fifths of the country. Angel Falls, at more than 3,200 feet the world's highest, is located in the Guayana highlands not far from Cerro Bolívar, an incredible mountain of almost pure iron ore.

Seven cities in Venezuela have more than one hundred thousand inhabitants, but none has equaled the fantastic level of urban development achieved in only a few decades by Caracas, the capital. Other cities are Maracaibo, the oil metropolis; Maracay, center of a rich farming area; Valencia, the most highly industrialized city; Ciudad Bolívar, formerly Angostura, site of the Congress of that name; La Guaira, the country's major port, and, finally, the progressive city of Barquisimeto.

**History.** On August 1, 1498, Columbus discovered the territory later to be called Venezuela when he dropped anchor in the Gulf of Paria. His report of the gold and pearls to be found in these lands prompted Alonso de Ojeda and Amerigo Vespucci to explore the Caribbean coast as far as Lake Maracaibo. The shores of Venezuela soon became famous for their pearls. One of the first European communities in the New World was Cumaná, founded in 1520 on the Caribbean.

Caracas, founded in 1567, became the capital in 1577. During the first half of the sixteenth century, New Andalucía, comprising most of the eastern part of Venezuela, was under the jurisdiction of the Audiencia of Santo Domingo; it was subsequently incorporated into the Viceroyalty of New Granada (Colombia). In 1777, the Captaincy General of the United Provinces of Venezuela was established with the same boundaries as the present republic, and in 1786 the Royal Audiencia of Caracas was formed. The many civilian and military leaders contributed by Venezuela to the cause of emancipation include two of outstanding historical status: Francisco de Miranda, the forefather of the independence movement, and Simón Bolívar, the Liberator. On July 5, 1811, the Constituent Congress of Venezuela declared its independence from Spain, and enacted a new constitution at the end of that year. The royalist forces regained control of the country shortly thereafter, but in 1821 they were decisively defeated by the patriots in the Battle of Carabobo. The political genius of Bolívar then forged Gran Colombia from the Republics of Venezuela, New Granada, Ecuador, and what is today the Republic of Panama, with the Liberator as President. In 1830, Venezuela separated from Gran Colombia and adopted its own Constitution.

Venezuela gave to America not only a great general whose military genius won the freedom of half a continent, but also a statesman who was a century ahead of his time in the field of international relations. As early as 1815, Bolívar promoted the idea of a "league of nations of the New World," and to this end he convoked the now historic Congress of Panama in 1826. Although the Treaty of Confederation which the delegates of the various republics signed did not endure, it embodied Bolívar's concepts of collective security and the peaceful settlement of dispute by arbitration and conciliation. These principles, radical in their days, became the cornerstone of the inter-American system and are put into practice today by the Organization of American States.

Many years after the Liberator, in 1908, Juan Vicente Gómez seized power and set up a dictatorial regime that was to last until 1935. It must be acknowledged that it was during this period that the oil fields were discovered and the nation first became prosperous. The Acción Democrática party won the elections of 1947, installing as President the great novelist Rómulo Gallegos, who was ousted by a military coup. Marcos Pérez Jiménez held power until 1958, when he was succeeded by Rómulo Betancourt, who set the country on its present course of an orderly succession of democratic administrations. Rafael Caldera was elected president in 1968.

**Culture.** As in other parts of the Caribbean, the colonial economy imported contingents of Negro slaves, while the rising prosperity of the past few decades attracted a wave of immigrants. The **llanero** is perhaps the most authentic figure in the country's past. His participation in the struggles for independence was both heroic and decisive. It was Bolívar's teacher, Simón Rodríquez, who marked the emergence of a liberal and enlightened trend which, despite the economic and political conditions prevailing during the nineteenth century and early in the twentieth, was to produce such notable exponents as Andres Bello, famous throughout the Hemisphere; Rufino

Blanco Fonbona; the poet Antonio Pérez Bonalde; and Cecilio Acosta. A strong movement toward national identity is apparent in both literature and art. Novelists Uslar Pietri and especially Rómulo Gallegos, author of **Doña Bárbara**, achieved international fame. Mario Picón Salas made an impressive contribution to historical criticism, while in the field of science Arnoldo Babaldón helped to eradicate malaria from the country. Martín Tovar and Arturo Michelena promoted the nationalistic trend in painting, which is carried on today by many fine local artists. Jesús Soto is a leader in the modern kinetic art movement.

Venezuelan folk arts are derived from the nation's three cultural sources: Indian, Spanish, and African. The rhythmic **joropo** is popular throughout the Americas.

**Economy.** Manufacturing now accounts for nearly one fifth of GNP, rivalling mining and petroleum in its importance to the economy. Principal industries are food processing, petroleum refining, beverages, vehicles and parts, chemicals, clothing, and textiles. After petroleum and petroleum products, the main exports are iron ore, coffee and cocoa.

*As it looks to the future,
Latin America preserves its rich
colonial heritage. Organ in
La Merced church,
Quito, Ecuador.*

# INDEX

# INDEX